中国科幻小说精选·中英对照

月光岛
MOONLIGHT ISLAND

金涛 著

温绍贤 译

[英]蒂娜·巴莱 审校

科学普及出版社

·北京·

图书在版编目（CIP）数据

月光岛：中英对照/金涛著；温绍贤译．—北京：科学普及出版社，2014.6

（中国科幻小说精选）

ISBN 978-7-110-08627-8

Ⅰ．①月… Ⅱ．①金… ②温… Ⅲ．①英语—汉语—对照读物 ②儿童文学—科学幻想小说—作品集—中国—当代 Ⅳ．①H319.4：I

中国版本图书馆CIP数据核字(2014)第096621号

出 版 人	苏　青
责任编辑	单　亭　张　莉
封面设计	银搏时代
责任校对	王勤杰
责任印制	张建农

出　　版	科学普及出版社
发　　行	科学普及出版社发行部
地　　址	北京市海淀区中关村南大街16号
邮　　编	100081
发行电话	010-62173865
传　　真	010-62179148
网　　址	http://www.cspbooks.com.cn

开　　本	880mm × 1230mm　1/32
字　　数	68千字
印　　张	5.25
印　　数	1—5000册
版　　次	2014年8月第1版
印　　次	2014年8月第1次印刷
印　　刷	北京盛通印刷股份有限公司
书　　号	ISBN 978-7-110-08627-8 / H · 212
定　　价	18.00元

关于月光岛

《月光岛》最初在哈尔滨出版的《科学时代》（主编刘沙）1980年第一期和第二期连载。

1980年发行全国的《新华月报》（文摘版）第7期转载《月光岛》。该期《新华月报》同时发表著名科幻作家郑文光对《月光岛》的评价文章《要正视现实——喜读金涛同志的科学幻想小说〈月光岛〉》，以及香港作家杜渐的论文《谈中国科学小说创作中的一些问题》（原载香港《开卷》1980年第10期）。

1981年3月，《月光岛》和作者另一篇科幻小说《沼地上的木屋》结集，由地质出版社出版（责任编辑叶冰如）。

1998年10月，在初版过了17年之后，上海科技教育出版社出版一套“绘图科幻精品丛书”，将《月光岛》改编后收入这套丛书，印了10 000册。

2009年四川《科幻世界》30周年特别纪念（1979—2009），将《月光岛》评为“中国科幻三十年九大经典短篇”之一。全文收入《科幻世界》30周年特别纪念增刊。

2009年5月，湖北少年儿童出版社出版《月光岛》，与作者的另一部科幻小说《马小哈奇遇记》合为一集，纳入该社的“科普名人名著书系”。

CONTENTS

目录

灯塔管理员

初秋的一个黄昏，落日余晖在大海的胸膜上披上了一件五彩斑斓的美丽罩衣，这时，有个二十来岁的年轻人默默地沿着一级级的石条蹬道，向月光岩的顶上攀去。他钻进一座高高耸立在月光岩上的灯塔。不大会儿工夫，一道白光从灯塔顶部的玻璃窗孔迸射出来，预告着黑夜来临了。

这个年轻人走出灯塔，伫立在悬崖边缘。他眯缝着眼睛，向落日沉没的远方凝视了很久。从那灼热的目光和一双紧闭的嘴唇上可以看出他似乎在期待着什么。然而在视线所及的海面，除了十几只在苍茫暮色中鼓噪的信天翁，成双结队地在海滩附近徘徊外，海上空无一物。不一会儿，最后一抹玫瑰色的晚霞余晖也从天际消失了。

他沿原路走下月光岩，回到他住的屋子，这是一幢临近海边的简陋石屋。他心烦意乱地闷坐在黑洞洞的房里，电灯也忘记拧开，陷入深沉的思索中……

他叫梅生，四年前从东南海洋大学海洋生物化学系毕

THE LIGHTHOUSE KFEPER

It was an evening in early autumn. The sun had recently set, and while the surface of the sea still glowed with the reflected gorgeous colour of the sky, a young man at his mid twenties climbed a long flight of rocky steps towards a lighthouse, high on top of the Moon Cliff. When he reached the lighthouse he disappeared inside it. Before long, a bright beam of light shone from its top glass-window, signaling that night had fallen.

When the young man emerged from the lighthouse again, he stood for a long time on the edge of the cliff, staring with narrowed eyes at the distant horizon, where the sky was still red. With his mouth tightly closed, he had an earnestly expectant look in his eyes, yet the wide expanse of sea over which he gazed showed nothing except a dozen of albatrosses near the beach at the foot of the cliff, circling in pairs, their harsh cries reaching him through the dusk. Then the last tinges of rosy colour slowly faded from the horizon.

The young man at last retraced his way down the steps from the Moon Cliff to his house. It was a simple stone house near the seashore. Inside, he sat silently in the dark, too preoccupied with his own thoughts and problems to remember to put the light on.

He was called Mei Sheng. He had graduated from the Southeast Oceanographical Institute four years before, but

业。那年夏天，一场比十二级台风还要猛烈千百倍的政治风暴，汪洋恣肆地席卷了九百六十万平方公里的大地。梅生这个毫无生活阅历的年轻大学生，像初次出海的水手，驾着一叶四处漏水的独木舟，在狂风恶浪中挣扎。不过比起和他同时代的青年人，他毕竟幸运得多。就在他惊魂未定时，不知来自何方的一股洋流推动他的小舟，把他送到荒凉的月光岛上，从此他开始了灯塔管理员的生活。

他确实是最合适不过的人选。他是个孤儿，是人民用乳汁把他哺养成人的。在旁人眼里看来，灯塔管理员的工作比起囚犯好不了多少，这里缺乏起码的物质生活和文化娱乐，唯一和世界的联系是每隔半个月航运局给他送来粮食和蔬菜的运输船，然而，他却深深爱上了荒凉的月光岛，也很满意他所从事的这个工作。

他是个天生喜欢和大自然为伍的人。刚来的那些日子，他简直像个头一回逛动物园的孩子，成天在岛屿周围，在丛林密集的山岩，在洁白如银的沙滩跑个不停。他一会儿像条鲮鱼划开碧蓝碧蓝的海水，遨游在绚丽多彩的海底；

that same summer people's life had been driven violently out of its expected course by the political storms hundreds of times more violent than a force 12 typhoon. In the turmoil which then engulfed the whole vast country, Mei Sheng, a young graduate with little experience in life – was like a sailor going to sea for the first time, adrift in a leaky canoe, struggling against a fierce wind and angry waves. In the event, however, he was more fortunate than many of his contemporaries; his canoe had been carried by a mysterious ocean current to this desolate job when he was still badly shaken and ever since he had been the lighthouse keeper on Moonlight Island.

The position suited him in many ways. He was an orphan, brought up in state institutions. To many people, the life of a lighthouse keeper would have been no better than that of a prisoner: there was no cultural life, existence was harsh, and his only contact with the outside world was the cargo ship sent by the Shipping Bureau which brought him food supplies every fortnight. But he was content with the work, and had grown to love Moonlight Island.

He had always been fascinated by nature. During the first weeks after his arrival he was simply like a child in paradise. He spent long hours traveling the places round the island, the cliffs in the thick forests, and the beach of silvery sand. He swam like a mullet, breaking up the blue water, or dived down

一会儿像只懒洋洋的海豹，仰卧在灼热的沙滩上，让热带的阳光炙烤他那一身古铜色的、充满青春活力的皮肤。他还花了整整一个来月的时间，对自己将要长期定居的环境作了一番认真的科学调查，把调查结果详详细细地写入他的笔记本：

“月光岛”——多么动听的名字！——是更新世一次海底火山爆发的产物，从岛上火山堆积物（主要成分是玄武岩）的结构和层次判断，它露出海面的时间不超过五万年。岛上的制高点，那座突兀高峻的月光岩海拔高达172.4米，是当初喷吐熔岩的火山锥。岛屿面积为0.95平方千米，距陆地最近距离为11.57海里[①]。植物种类估计近百种，主要为桃金娘科、棕榈科、兰科、大戟科、番石榴科。动物种属不详，待查。

岛上灯塔根据建筑标记，是第二次世界大战时日本海军东亚舰队七十五军团所建。

全岛共有居民三十六人，岛屿西部有一座渔村，渔民

① 1海里=1852米。

to the gorgeous seabed, or lay like a languid seal on the hot beach, his skin tanning in the tropical sun which made him feel the full range of his youth and vigour. He also spent a whole month conducting a serious scientific survey of the island, and some details from his notebook give a concise description of the new place where he would stay for a long time to come:

> Moonlight Island (a suitably beautiful name) is the result of a submarine volcanic eruption in the Pleistocene Epoch. Judging by the structure and layers of volcanic accumulation (of which the main element is basalt), it is less than fifty thousand years since the island emerged from the sea. The highest point of the island, the towering steep cliff with an elevation of 172.4 metres, is the top of the volcano which erupted at that time. The area of the island is 0.95 square kilometres, and the nearest distance to the mainland is 11.57 nautical miles. There are estimated to be about 100 species of plants, mostly Myrtaceae, Palmae, Orchidaceae, Euphorbiaceae, and Psidium guajava. The species and genera of the island's animals are unknown, and have yet to be surveyed.
>
> According to the inscriptions on it, the lighthouse on the island was built by the 75th Army Group of the East Asian Fleet of the Japanese Navy during World War II.
>
> There is a population of 36 people on the island. There is a fishing village in the western part, where the fisher folk live a

过着与世隔绝的生活。他们是什么时候迁入月光岛的，没有人知道。最令人费解的是，渔村没有小孩，一个也没有，只有二十五个男人，十个女人，也许是由于这里环境艰苦，他们把孩子们安置在别的什么地方，但也无从证实。至于海岛东部，唯一的居民是灯塔管理员……

不过，年轻的大学生安心在月光岛上生活还另有原因。在大学，他勤奋刻苦，一丝不苟，深得生物化学家孟凡凯教授的垂青。他的毕业论文便是在孟教授的直接指导下完成的，说得准确一些，这是他们师生合作的一项科研课题。不幸的是，这项重大的科研项目刚进入实验阶段，孟教授在一次意想不到的事件中身陷囹圄，至今下落不明；接着梅生离开了大学，来到了几乎与世隔绝的孤岛。

气象学家发现盛行在南中国海和孟加拉国湾的台风，有个极为有趣的现象：台风中心，有个台风眼。尽管台风经过的地方的天气是遮天蔽日的狂风暴雨，小小的台风眼却依然风平浪静，天晴日朗。在风狂雨骤的那些年月，月光岛正

life isolated from the outside world. No one seems to know when they came to the island. One thing that has puzzled me is that there are no children; just 25 men and 10 women. Perhaps they send their children somewhere else, as the life is very hard here. However, I cannot confirm this. In the east part of the island, the only living being is the lighthouse keeper...

There was an additional reason for Mei Sheng to be contented with his position on the island. At the Institute of Oceanography he had been an extremely able and hard-working student, and had caught the attention of Professor Meng Fankai, an eminent biochemist. Mei Sheng's final thesis at the Institute was conducted under Professor Meng's supervision, but in fact it was the record of a piece of research which was being conducted jointly by himself and Professor Meng. However, at a crucial point in their research project of great importance, when they were about to start a series of experiments to test their theories, the storm had hit them. Out of the blue it had sent Professor Meng to prison – Mei Sheng knew neither why nor where – and Mei Sheng himself to his lonely life on the island.

Meteorologists have discovered that there was a very interesting phenomenon in the typhoons often seen in the South China Sea and the Bay of Bengal. They have at their very centre a "typhoon eye": all around, as the storm passes, the typhoon completely blots out the sky, but under the small typhoon eye the weather is sunny and the sea is calm. To Mei

是这样一个平静的台风眼。

梅生始终没有忘记他和孟教授合作的课题。他打心眼里爱上了“台风眼”，爱上了这里的宁静和自由。的确，没有人愿意涉足这儿来过问他的工作，似乎也没有人注意到他这个游离在风暴之外的漏网之鱼。他在卧室隔壁一间堆放杂物的贮藏室里，精心布置了一间再简陋不过的实验室。四年的光阴就这样流逝了，他忘情地从事着这项课题的对比实验，积累了将近一千页的实验记录。他朦胧地意识到，一个惊人的结论，像黎明的曙光一样在这间陋室里快要诞生了……

但是，在这个节骨眼上，实验被迫中断了，整整中断了半个月。

他逮住了一只活蹦乱跳的金丝猴，那是半个月前发生的事。他高兴得喘不过气来，小心翼翼地把这个毛茸茸的小馋鬼关进铁笼。一个成熟的念头在他的头脑里油然而生，他决定在这只难以觅求的灵长目高等动物身上进行一次难度最大的实验。他记得有一次孟教授用低沉的声调对他说：

Sheng, Moonlight Island was a peaceful typhoon eye amidst the fierce whirl of the political storms during that time.

He did not, however, forget their joint project. He had come to love this “typhoon eye” from the bottom of his heart, had come to love the tranquility and freedom of Moonlight Island. As a matter of fact no one would like to come to inspect what he did here; it seemed neither was there any one who took any notice of him who was like a fish that has escaped from the net. So he turned the storeroom by his bedroom into a simple but meticulously arranged laboratory, and for four years he had been completely absorbed in the project, conducting comparative experiments which he had planned, and now he had written nearly a thousand pages of notes, and he was vaguely conscious that these experiments, conducted in one humble room in a shabby little house, really were leading to the most astounding conclusion, which might be seen as a moment in history.

Just at the moment he was forced to be idle, because for two weeks – with the end of his work nearly in reach – he had had to suspend all experiments.

A fortnight ago he had managed to capture a golden monkey, and he was keeping the lively gluttonous little creature securely in an iron cage. This stroke of luck gave him an opportunity which made him breathless with excitement. A mature idea welled up in his mind. He decided to perform the most difficult experiment on one of the higher primates, which was an opportunity hard to come by. He had never forgotten a conversation with Professor Meng one day, “Remember,” the

“记住，我们的最终目的是揭开人类死亡之谜。一切动物的实验都不能代替人体本身的试验。全部困难恰恰在于这点，因为我们很难实现人体的实验，这不仅要冒极大的风险，而且是科学所不允许的。”

“那该怎么办？”他询问自己的老师。

“我想，如果能用灵长目动物作为实验材料，我们至少可以接近真理一步，”孟教授深凹的眼窝里闪动着智慧的光芒，“这样的话，我准备下一步请你在我的身体上做最后一个对比实验，我相信我们的结论是正确的！”

“你……用你的身体？”梅生几乎惊叫起来。

“为什么不可以呢？每个献身科学的人都应该随时有这种准备，”教授的嘴角浮现一丝微笑，接着他向自己的学生谈起人类历史上许多献身科学的大无畏的勇士，他讲到布鲁诺、富兰克林、居里夫人、塞尔维特……

孟教授的谈话对年轻的大学生印象太深刻了。为了做好这次实验，他花了几个通宵拟定了实验方案，对各种可能出现的意外都制定了措施。

Professor had said, in a low voice, “that since our final goal is to unveil the secret of the death of humans, ultimately we will need to experiment on a human being; experiments on animals can never be enough. Here lies our difficulty, for we can’t experiment on people – the risk is too great, and good scientific practice forbids it.”

“Then how do we get round the problem?” Mei Sheng had asked his teacher.

“I think if we conduct our experiment on a primate, we will at least be a step nearer to the truth.” Then Professor Meng’s deep-set eyes had glowed, and he had continued, “In that case, I intend to ask you to make the next experiment on me, as the final proof – convinced, as I am, that our conclusions are correct.”

“On you — but your life would be at risk!” Mei Sheng had cried out in alarm.

“Why not? Anyone who devotes himself to science should be ready to sacrifice everything to it.” A faint smile had appeared at the corner of his mouth, and he had gone on to tell his student about the many brave fighters who had devoted themselves whole-heartedly to science in the history of mankind. He talked about Bruno, Franklin, Maria Sklodowska Curie, Michael Servetus and many others.

Mei Sheng, this young college graduate, had been tremendously impressed by his Professor’s words. Now in order to do a good job in this experiment, he had spent several sleepless and excited nights as he worked out the details of the experiment and tried to anticipate every possible mishap.

接着，他走向屋角的一只木柜，那是储存化学药品及各种试剂的专柜。他兴冲冲地拉开柜门，蓦地，他气恼地把门"砰"地关上，颓然地倒在椅子上。糟糕透了，药品全部用光。甭说一只金丝猴，连解剖一只苍蝇也远远不够。他只好放下试验，掏出全部积蓄，给出海的渔民开了一张满是拉丁文的购货清单……

不知过了多久，一弯新月从月光岩的顶巅冉冉升起。水银似的月光穿过窗前一株棕榈的扇形树冠，斑斑点点泻在床前的地板上。潮水自远而近，在窗脚的礁石上轰然作响，仿佛憋足了气力要掀掉屹立在岭岩上的石屋。

梅生伸手打开电灯。他取下墙上挂着的一件夹克，打算到渔村探听一下渔轮的确切消息。就在这时，窗外传来他盼望已久的喊声："梅生——"

梅生撂下衣服，敏捷地奔到窗前，探头向外张望。

朦胧的月光下，一艘黑乎乎的船体贴着窗下的石壁缓缓移动，像一只甲虫在波光闪烁着的海面划出一条长长的、清晰的曲线。船上有人高声唤他："喂，快来！"

He went to the corner cupboard where he stored chemicals excitedly, only to start back with surprise. In his first disappointment he had banged the cupboard door shut and then slumped dejectedly in a chair. What bad luck! The chemicals were all used up. There weren't enough chemicals to work on a fly, let alone a golden monkey. There was no choice but to put aside the experiment for the time being. He had given all his savings, and a shopping list full of Latin words, to one of the fishermen who regularly visited the mainland...

The days passed, and a new moon rose over the top of the cliff, its silvery light on the foot of Mei Sheng's bed broken into strange patterns by the fan-shaped crown of a palm tree outside his bedroom window. The incoming tide flung breakers against the beach only a few yards away, as though it had hopes of demolishing the little stone house on the cliff.

Mei Sheng turned on the light, and took down a warm jacket, for tonight he intended to go to the fishing village to see if there was any news of the fishing boat. But just at that moment, the voice that he had been waiting for shouted from the darkness outside.

"Mei Sheng —"

Mei Sheng dropped the jacket and rushed to the window. He leant out and looked round.

In the dim moonlight he could see the dark beetle-like shape of a boat moored by the rocks at one end of the beach below his house. It was clearly outlined against the glimmering waves. Someone on the boat called him again in a loud voice: "Hello, Mei Sheng! Please come quickly!"

不错，是他们！梅生含糊地应了一句，兴奋地拔腿跑去。他听得很真，喊他的是那个诨号叫海狼的老渔夫。他飞也似地跳下门前的石阶，向前奔去。

海狼老爹迎上前来，把一只方方正正、还用绳子捆得挺结实的纸箱塞在他的手里。

“给你，”他嘟哝着说，“这玩意儿真不好买，跑了好儿家都说没货，最后还是托我的表弟走了后门，到化工仓库里才把药品配齐……”

梅生接过纸箱，忙不迭地道谢。

“谢什么！”海狼老爹吼了起来，皱着眉头，说：“以后少说这些见外的话，我不爱听！”

梅生尴尬地笑笑：“老爹，坐一会儿吧，还有大半瓶五加皮。外面最近有些什么新闻，给我讲讲……”

梅生说到这儿，突然戛然而止。他发觉海狼老爹的反应极为冷淡。老渔夫忧心忡忡，两手对搓，面部表情在月光下显得分外严峻。

“出了什么事？”梅生不安地问，“难道渔船在海上

It was the fishing boat! Mei Sheng shouted back in a hoarse voice, and then dashed outside. He clearly recognized it was the voice of Sea Wolf, the nickname of an old fisherman to whom he had given his shopping list.

As he ran towards the boat, he met Sea Wolf, who was carrying a square cardboard box securely tied with a string.

"Here you are," said Sea Wolf, giving him the box. "These things weren't easy to get. I went to several chemists without any success, but then at last I asked my cousin to use his influence to help me, and he managed to find everything you want through the chemical warehouse where he works."

Mei Sheng, clutching the cardboard box, thanked Sea Wolf profusely.

"Don't thank me!" Sea Wolf growled, glaring amiably at Mei Sheng. "I shall be offended if you treat me like a stranger!"

Mei Sheng was a little embarrassed, but smiled and continued: "Uncle Sea Wolf, would you like to come into the house? I've kept more than half a bottle of wine of slender acanthopanax bark. And you can tell me what has been going on recently in the world outside..."

Mei Sheng suddenly stopped, for he realized that Sea Wolf was barely listening. The old fisherman looked very anxious; he was rubbing his hands together, and in the moonlight his expression seemed unusually grave.

"What's happened?" he asked uneasily. "Has there been

出了事故，是不是哪个渔民遇难了……”他的脑子里闪电似地胡思乱想。

海狼老爹吞吞吐吐，一双忧郁的眼睛在他的脸上足足打量了好几分钟。

“老爹，你是怎么啦？”梅生紧跑了几步，和海狼老爹前后脚走进房内。

海狼老爹拖来一把凳子，坐在靠窗口不远的地方，慢吞吞地掏出烟斗。当他划着火柴，突然他从凳子上站起来走到过道里，朝那间“实验室”瞅了一眼。“我想打听件事情，梅生，你实话告诉我，你的那个把死鱼救活的办法，究竟能不能救……救人？”听得出来，他的声音微微有些颤抖。

梅生越发感到莫名其妙。呆了半晌，他的嘴里才断断续续冒出几个字：“谁？到……底……是谁？”

海狼老爹见他脸色骤变，连忙向他说明：“你别紧张，不是我们这儿的人。”没等梅生开口，他又急迫地问：“到

an accident with the boat? Has someone on board died?" He tried to guess what might be the matter.

Sea Wolf did not answer, but stood gazing at Mei Sheng for what seemed a long time.

"Uncle, what's the matter with you?" Mei Sheng asked, as he followed Sea Wolf into the house.

Sea Wolf dragged a stool to the side of the window and slowly took out his pipe. But then when he had struck a match, he suddenly got up again, and walked out of the room into Mei Sheng's laboratory, and stood looking round it. "I want to ask you something, Mei Sheng. Please tell me honestly: does your method for bringing a dead fish to life work on ... on a human being?" Mei Sheng could hear his voice trembling.

Mei Sheng was even more startled at this, and just stammered disjointedly, "Who...What...Do you mean?"

Seeing his anxiety, Sea Wolf tried to set his mind at ease, saying, "Don't worry, nothing is wrong with any of our people here." Then before Mei Sheng could speak, he again asked eagerly, "Does your method work on human beings?"

底行不行？”

梅生心里的一块石头落了地，如释重负地舒了口气。他十分为难。在这个孤岛上，只有海狼老爹一个人知道他的试验，那是一次无意中被他发现的。不过能不能把死人救活，他没有试验过，这些深奥的道理也无法三言两语对海狼老爹讲清楚。他用手挠挠头，面有难色地说道：“老爹，不瞒您说，医生不见病人是无法开方下药的，你叫我怎么说呢？”

海狼老爹一时没有作声，低着头猛吸了几口烟。过了片刻，他磕掉烟斗中的灰烬，终于把事情的原委说了出来。

“是这么回事。天刚黑下来的时候，我们已经看见了月光岛模模糊糊的轮廓，估计距离月光岛顶多只有十几里光景。这时忽然在渔船的左前方出现一片刀鱼群，密密麻麻，连海水都变了色。我们当然不肯轻易放过这个送上门的好机会，再说船舱还空着一半哩。于是我们围着这片海区兜了个大弯，足足忙了两个多钟头。等我们收完网具，月亮已经升得老高老高了。”

Mei Sheng was relieved to hear that his friends were safe, but at a loss to know what to answer. On the island, Sea Wolf was the only person who knew about the experiments, which he discovered only accidentally. But his experiments had not yet reached the stage where he could give any assurance that the method could bring someone back to life. It was impossible to explain everything to Sea Wolf in a few words. He scratched his head, and said hesitantly: "I tell you honestly, Uncle, a doctor can't write out a prescription without seeing the patient. What do you expect me to say?"

Sea Wolf was silent, and stood with his head bowed, smoking vigorously, for a while. Then he knocked the ashes out of his pipe, and then told him the whole story:

"It's like this. We were on our way home. By the time we could see Moonlight Island in distance, it was getting dark. I reckon our boat was about ten odd miles off still. All of a sudden we came on a huge shoal of mullet – there were so many of them that they made the sea change colour. Well, of course we couldn't let the chance of such a haul slip – especially as our hold was half empty – so we circled round and lowered the nets. We were more than two hours at it. By the time we finished, the moon was high in the sky."

海狼老爹把凳子向梅生这边挪近些："事情怪就怪在这儿。渔船靠了岸，伙计们盼家心切，一个个走光了。我瞅着你这箱药品，知道你等着要用，决定先上你这儿来，顺便带几条新鲜鱼给你尝尝鲜。我扒开甲板舱口的铁盖，猫着腰把胳膊伸了进去。呀，好凉！鱼群裹着一块块人造冰哩。我用手在舱里东摸一把，西抓一把，里面漆黑一团，什么也看不见，忽然我的手摸着一个软绵绵的东西。'噢，这是个啥玩意？'我心里挺纳闷，这不像海蜇，也不是乌贼，细长细长，还挺软和，我索性俯下上半截身体，把脑袋伸进舱口，顺着那个柔软的东西往前摸了过去……"

梅生见海狼老爹说得绘声绘色，叫人心里发毛，忍不住问道："到底摸到了什么？"

海狼老爹一双惊恐的眼睛睁得老大，他向左右瞥了一眼，然后贴近梅生的耳朵，悄悄地说了几个字。话音刚落，梅生腾地从床上蹦起来，大惊失色地说："你真的看清楚了？"

"这还有假，的的确确是一具尸体，而且还是个女人！"

Sea Wolf moved his stool nearer to Mei Sheng: "Then it happened. When the boat pulled in to shore, my partners were eager to get home, so they made straight for the village. As I knew you were waiting for these chemicals, I decided to come here first. I wanted to bring you some fresh fish by the way, so I lifted the iron hatch away from the hold, and bent over and stretched my arm inside. It was freezing cold in there, as the fish are packed in artificial ice. I had my arm right in, feeling here and there. It was very dark in the hold, and I couldn't see anything. Suddenly I touched something soft. 'What's this?' I wondered. It wasn't like jelly fish, nor cuttlefish. It was long and slender and soft. I stooped down and put my head right into the mouth of the hold, and stretched forward to touch the soft thing again..."

Sea Wolf's description was so vivid that Mei Sheng felt a shiver run down his spine. He couldn't help asking, "And what was it?"

Sea Wolf opened his eyes very wide with fear. He looked round, and then got close to Mei Sheng's ear and murmured in a few words, which instantly made Mei Sheng jump up in astonishment. "Could you really see it properly?" he asked, horrified.

"No mistake about it. It really was a dead body. A woman "

“女人？”梅生不由地惊叫起来。

“嗯，不信，你自己去看看嘛！”

“在哪儿？”梅生气喘吁吁地问。

“就在门外，船上呀！”

“嘿，你怎么不早说，快带我去看看呀！”

几分钟后，这一老一少像一阵旋风似地跑到船上。

梅生的神情紧张极了。他弓着腰，壮着胆子钻进寒气逼人的冷藏舱。过了一会，抱出了一具尸体，刚巧，淡淡的月光迎面而来，把尸体的面部和全身照得清晰极了。在这一瞬间，梅生和海狼老爹异口同声地惊叫起来：“呀！”

他们看得再清楚不过了。纠缠粘连的乌黑长发，清秀瘦削的面容，紧贴身体的单薄的连衣裙，裸露的脚踝和浅黄色的人造丝袜……原来死者是个只有十八九岁的少女！

他们默默地对视了一眼，谁也不想开口。海狼老爹只觉得鼻子一阵酸楚。苦涩的泪水在他那被海风吹得红肿的眼眶里直打转转，喃喃地说：“可怜，真是造孽啊……”

梅生的脸色变得铁青，阴沉的目光默默凝视着万籁俱

"A woman?" Mei Sheng cried in fear.

"Well, if you don't believe me, come and have a look for yourself!"

"Where is it?" Mei Sheng asked, panting.

"In the hold of the boat still."

"Good heavens, why didn't you say so earlier? Quick, take me there!"

Minutes later, the two men, old and young, tore out of the house like a whirlwind and then stood on the deck of the boat.

Mei Sheng was exceedingly frightened, but nerved himself and bent over and got right inside the uncovered refrigerator hold. It was bitterly cold in there. A couple of minutes later he emerged, carrying a body in his arms. The moon was right overhead, and in its pale light they could see the corpse's face and form quite distinctly. They both exclaimed in horror at the same moment.

In fact they both felt they could see her only too clearly. Her long, jet black hair was all entangled. She had a pretty face, but thin and haggard-looking. She wore a thin, ragged dress, and her heels broke through her worn out yellow artificial silk stockings... She looked quite young – she must have been about 18 or 19 years old.

They stared at each other, neither was able to speak for a moment. Sea Wolf felt bitter tears welling up in his eyes, toughened though they were by the sea winds. He murmured, "Poor girl – what a tragedy..."

Mei Sheng's face was very pale. He looked away from the poor corpse and turned sad eyes to the utterly quiet surface of

寂的海面。这突如其来的悲惨景象使他的心房隐隐作痛。死者不像失足落水的，从她的衣着、脸部表情都可以看出。但是她是谁？这样的青春妙龄，为什么要走上这条绝路？谁也无法回答。梅生捧着这具尸体暗自思忖：“怎么办？把她重新抛到大海，然后让她从地球上永远消失，不留一丝痕迹？还是……”

“你倒是说话呀？”海狼老爹见梅生痴呆的神情，用胳膊肘捅了他一下，焦虑地问。

“嗯，”梅生从冥想中惊醒过来，“你没有告诉别人吧？”他向尸体努了努嘴。

海狼老爹会意地眨眨眼睛，答道：“除了你我，只有它知道。”他手指着头顶上的明月。

“试试看吧！”梅生咬着嘴唇，费了很大气力从牙缝里挤出这句话。他把这具无名尸体郑重地贴在他那温暖的胸膛上，像是从大海里拾到人间遗弃的珍宝，大踏步朝石屋走去。

月光如水，在他们身后不远的丛林里突然传来一声猿猴的哀鸣，声音悲凉而凄惶……

the sea silently. His heart felt sore at this tragedy, which appeared so suddenly. Her dress and expression suggested that this had been no accident. But who was she? Why should she commit suicide so young? There was no one to give him an answer. As he stood there, still holding the body, he debated with himself, “What shall I do? Throw her into the sea again, and let her vanish from this world forever without a trace? Or...”

Seeing Mei Sheng so silent, Sea Wolf shook him by the arm and asked anxiously, “Why don’t you say something?”

“Well,” Mei Sheng was awakened from his deep thought. “Have you told anyone else about her?” He pouted his lips at him, indicating the body.

Sea Wolf knew what he was getting at, and blinking his eyes he answered : “No. Apart from you and me, only she has seen her.” He pointed at the moon above their heads.

Mei Sheng bit his lip, and then eventually said, in a low voice but with great determination, “Let me try!” He pressed the unknown body solemnly against his warm breast, feeling that he had won from the sea a treasure abandoned by the world.

As he headed with long strides for the stone house, through a flood of translucent moonlight, there sounded all of a sudden the eerie, melancholy wail of a gibbon from the forest behind him not far away...

实 验

传说月亮和潮汐是一对热恋的情人，它们每月定期约会，诉说衷情。这天，月亮和潮汐又相会了。海湾里潮流激荡，奔腾；白花花的大浪在嶙峋的礁石上跳跃，欢笑，发出声震如雷的吼声……

但是，“实验室”里却静悄无声，唯有房顶一盏大灯散发出耀眼的光芒，比往常任何时候都显得格外明亮。不知从什么时候起，梅生迷迷糊糊瞌上了眼皮，靠在操作台的边沿上睡着了。

在这间充满静谧气氛的房里，科学和死神的搏斗正处在短兵相接的决战阶段，整个战役的胜败也许即刻就要揭晓了。靠墙临时用木板搭的一张单人床上，雪白的床单严严实实掩盖了一切，只是在上端露出毫无血色的半张脸，既无从窥视她的面容，也无法判断那里是否存在真实的生命。床头捆着一根指头粗细的竹竿，吊着一只透明玻璃瓶，一滴滴淡黄的液体从里面渗了出来，顺着一根细长的橡皮

THE EXPERIMENT

Legend has it that the moon and tide were once passionate lovers, and that once a month they still meet to open their hearts to each other. Tonight was the time for their monthly rendezvous. In the bay at the foot of the cliff the tide was at its height, and foaming white breakers surged against the reef in a cheerful merry mood with a noise like thunder...

In the laboratory in the little stone house, however, all was silent. A brighter bulb than formerly filled the room with dazzling light, but Mei Sheng, exhausted, had been dazed with sleep, leaning against the operating table.

In this extremely quiet room, the battle between science and death at close quarters was being carried out, and the final outcome of the battle might soon be known. The young woman's body lay on the makeshift operating table, securely covered over – except for her pale face – with a snow white sheet. It was neither impossible to tell her true countenance nor whether she was alive or not. From a bamboo pole as thick as a finger tied to the head of her bed of planks was suspended a transparent glass bottle, containing a yellow liquid. This liquid passed along a thin and long rubber tube,

管，伸进了白色的床单。

静，从未有过的安静。不过，倘若留神聆听，隐隐约约还有一阵阵“沙沙”声，来自操作台上，低微得令人难以觉察。

那是一口大玻璃缸，透明的玻璃盖下，成百上千的蚂蟥蠕动着。这些吸血鬼挤成一团，像泥鳅似地翻来覆去，攀爬，挣扎，互相践踏，不断从口腔分泌出淡黄色的汁液。轻微的“沙沙”声便是从这里传出来的。

这里进行的试验，神秘极了，也许只有梅生一个人才能解释。可是他实在太疲倦了。整整一个星期，他几乎没有睡过一个安稳觉。为了抢救这个死去的女子，他竭尽全力，把他的知识，他的才能，还有他和孟教授合伙研究的成果，一点不剩地用上了，可是结果究竟如何，他心里没有十分把握……

为了不打扰试验，海狼老爹尽量不上这边来。但是老渔夫实在难以控制自己，时常在夜深人静的时候跑来探听消息。这天黎明出海之前，他又在窗下出现了。

which disappeared under the sheet.

In the dead silence, it was just possible to hear a very faint rustling sound only with rapt attention, coming from a huge glass jar standing at the end of the operating table.

This large jar was full to the transparent glass brim with a slithering, wriggling mass of leeches. There were tens of hundreds of these bloodsuckers: the faint sounds were made by their continual movements as they squirmed round and over each other. It was the leeches that were secreting the light yellow fluid in the bottle.

Only Mei Sheng could have explained the mysterious course of this experiment. By now, however, he was almost too exhausted: for the sake of rescuing the dead woman, he had spent a week without a comfortable sleep, using all his skill and knowledge, and drawing on all his memories of the work done jointly by himself and Professor Meng. Yet despite all his efforts, he still felt uncertain as to the outcome...

During the week, Sea Wolf had done his best to refrain from coming to Mei Sheng's house, in order not to disturb him; but the old fisherman could not prevent himself, and several times appeared at dead of night to ask about the experiment. One morning at dawn, before his boat set out fishing, he had appeared under the window again, standing on tiptoe to look in.

“怎么样？有希望吗？”他踮起脚尖问道。

梅生打着哈欠，眼睛通红，又是一夜未眠。

他的神情有些焦躁不安，情况并不乐观。虽然经过努力，这个被死神夺走的女子，在第二天清晨，心脏就重新起搏，体温开始明显回升，肌体的肤色也由于血液通畅出现淡淡的血色，可是他并没有消除内心的疑虑。过去在许多动物身上做过的试验提醒他，这往往是死神要弄的骗人花招，果然，他的估计不错。

第四天清晨，女子的情况急剧恶化，她的呼吸变得非常微弱，滚烫的额头像烧红的炭火。梅生清楚地了解，在这个性命攸关的时刻，只要高烧不退，全部努力将会溃于一旦。不过他没有把这些告诉海狼老爹，也许是不想过于使老人失望，或者是他还不甘心在死神的威力下退却，他勉强地微笑着，对即将出海的老渔夫说：“放心吧，我是不达到目的誓不罢休的！”

“那就好，不过你自己也得注意，不要弄垮了。”老渔夫关照了几句。

"How goes it with the experiment? Is there still hope?"

Mei Sheng had yawned. His eyes were bloodshot, and it was evident that he had spent another sleepless night.

He had also looked very anxious. The experiment was not at that point progressing very well. His initial efforts had caused the dead woman's heart to start beating by the next morning; her temperature had gone up dramatically, and her skin had turned pink as her blood began to circulate again. However, he had known better than to rejoice at this stage: his many experiments on animals in the past warned him that this was often a trick played by the God of Death. And as he had expected, his forebodings were correct.

Early in the morning on the fourth day, the woman's condition had worsened rapidly. Her breathing became very feeble, and her forehead was hot to the touch. Mei Sheng had known that if he failed to bring down her fever at this juncture of life and death, all his efforts would be of no avail, but he had felt unable to tell Sea Wolf this. He did not want to disappoint the old man, nor was he yet resigned to retreating before the might of the God of Death. So he had forced a smile, and told the old fisherman as he was setting off for his daily fishing trip, "Please rest assured that I'll never give up until I succeed."

"Well said! But take care of yourself, and don't wear yourself out," the old man said a few kind words to him.

海狼老爹走后，梅生用冷水洗把脸，冷静地坐下来，把整个治疗方案从头至尾检查了一番。他翻开一张张观察记录，对抢救过程的每个细节都用怀疑的眼光重新加以审查，最后他恍然大悟了。

“对，应该这样！” 他蓦地拍了一下巴掌，兴奋地站起来，在屋子里激动地走来走去。

抢救过程中的明显错误，主要是药剂用量偏低，不敢超过理论计算公式的平均值。他没有充分估计到，试验材料不是一般的低等动物，而是实实在在的人。由于药量不够，这个女子的体内，生与死的因素一直处在抗衡状态，并且愈来愈恶化。看来这个公式还不够完整，它在应用于人体时要加一个参数。

“这个参数应该是……”他一面用铅笔在纸上迅速计算，一面翻看病历记录。当他算出最佳参数值时，他大胆地把药物浓度加大了一倍。他扎了一根竹竿，吊起了玻璃瓶，把定时注射改为点滴，这样一来，药物作用的效果好多了。他像个运筹帷幄的指挥官，探明了敌军防线的薄弱

After Sea Wolf had gone that morning, Mei Sheng had washed his face with cold water and sat down calmly to make a complete reassessment of his programme of medical treatment, from beginning to end. He had checked one observation after another, judging critically every detail of the course of the rescue. At last, he had suddenly seen the light:

"Yes of course, that's how I should do it!" Excitedly he had clapped his hands and begun to pace to and fro.

He had realized that his error in the course of the rescue must be mainly the size of the dosage. He had dared not use a dosage greater than the average produced by the formula he had worked out in his theoretical calculations, but he had failed fully to adjust for the fact that the object of the experiment this time was a human being, instead of a smaller animal. Because the dose he had used was too small, the factors of life and death were still fighting for control inside her body; if anything, her condition was now getting worse. Clearly, his formula was not quite right: an extra factor should be added to the calculation when the method was used on a human body.

"The extra factor should be..." He had scribbled rapidly on a bit of paper with a pencil, while looking back over his notes. Then, after rechecking all his calculations, he had made the bold decision to double the quantity of the medicine. He had found a bamboo pole and hung a glass bottle from it, changing from regular injections to an intravenous drip in order to make the action of the medicine more effective. He had felt like a general, directing strategies from a command tent, who decides promptly to dispatch his crack troops as soon

环节，当机立断地把最精锐的部队投入战场，由被动防守转入了战略性的总攻击了……

然而，这个大胆的方案对他来说，毕竟是第一次。他担心药物过猛会带来意想不到的副作用，甚至会产生无法挽回的突发性死亡。他带着这样无穷的忧虑进入了梦乡，他的脑子仍在不停地苦苦思索……思索……

忽然，“水……水……”梅生的耳膜“嗡嗡”了一阵。处于半睡眠状态的中枢神经突然亢奋起来。这声音仿佛是从遥远的宇宙空间传来的，微弱得像一线极细的金属丝，飘拂空中，忽高忽低。梅生平时难得听见人们说话的声音，他的听觉因而训练得非常敏锐。当这种微弱的声音出现不到几秒钟，梅生蓦地惊醒过来，敏捷地直奔床前，伸出了手……

“谢天谢地，成功了！……”他的手接触到女子的前额，冰凉冰凉，还有一层粘手的、茸毛似的薄汗。他不禁失声地叫了起来，眼睛顿时变得模糊起来，一行温暖的苦涩液体淌进他的口腔……这个男子汉有生以来第一回热

as he sees a weak point in the enemy's line of defence; at last he was able to unfold a general strategic offensive, instead of merely holding a defensive position...

However, he had never used this bold plan of attack before, and he greatly feared that too much of the medicine would produce unexpected side effects, or would lead to a sudden death, which this time would be irreversible. Tormented by these worries, he had fallen asleep in the laboratory, still thinking very hard of the problem in his dream.

Suddenly, his sleep was penetrated by a voice. "Water... water..." it said. It seemed to come from outer space; it was so feeble. It was like a very thin metal thread, drifting in the air – now high, now low. Mei Sheng's hearing was extremely sharp after his years on the island, and the feeble sound woke him with a start. He went quickly to the head of the operating table, and stretched out his hand...

"Thank goodness, it's working!..." When his hand touched her forehead, he felt that it was cooler, and that there was a thin film of moisture on it. In his relief tears blurred his eyes and rolled down his cheeks: it was the first time he had ever

泪滚滚，无法自禁。

他用颤抖的手拔掉女子手背上的针头，现在这已是多余的了。接着他取来一只盛满饮料的玻璃杯，给复苏的生命补充养料。

那个女子的眼睛还没有睁开，她大口大口地吸吮着，像初生的婴儿贪婪地吸吮母亲的奶汁，一杯饮料很快喝光了。过了一会儿，她的眼皮好像感受到灯光的刺激，微微跳动。梅生屏声敛息，像产妇第一次见到自己的婴儿，心中充满忐忑不安而又难以自禁的喜悦。

大约过了十来分钟，也许更长一些，那一对长睫毛的大眼睛终于挣脱了死神布下的黑暗罗网，慢慢地睁开了。不过，这双刚刚恢复视觉的眼睛交织着复杂极了的种种神情：惊骇、恐惧、悲哀、痛苦甚至还有点仇视的情绪。只有对人生绝望的人才会投射这样的目光。

“你别害怕……”梅生含笑地望着她，竭力想减轻她的恐惧心理。他轻轻摸着她的额头，不料她像只受惊的兔子，猛地推开梅生的手，全身蜷缩一团，用充满敌意的目

shed tears of joy. He simply could not help it.

He carefully removed the needles from the back of the woman's hand, his own hands trembling. They were unnecessary now. Then he fetched her a drink full of protein and vitamins to help her in her return to life.

She had not yet opened her eyes, but she drank greedily, like a new-born baby sucking its mother's milk – one big mouthful after another. She quickly drained the glass. Then it seemed that the light was beginning to reach her eyes – her eyelids fluttered lightly. Mei Sheng watched her with bated breath; he felt like a woman giving birth, catching a first glimpse of her baby. His heart was very full, with both happiness and uneasiness which he could hardly control.

About a quarter of an hour passed before she managed to break through the net of darkness cast by the God of Death and opened her eyes. She had big eyes, with long lashes. As they slowly opened, they reflected a variety of expressions – fear, sorrow, pain, and even a trace of hostility. Only those who have given up all hope in life have such an expression of despair in their eyes.

"Don't be afraid..." Mei Sheng smiled at her, trying to soothe her fears. He touched her lightly on the forehead, but she reacted like a frightened rabbit, and pushing away his hand, she huddled herself up and stared vigilantly at him with

光警戒着。

过了片刻，她突然喊道："你是谁？这是什么地方？"这是她重返人间的第一句话。

"安静一点，姑娘，不要害怕，这里没有人会伤害你……"梅生后退一步，笑容可掬地安慰她。但是，这个女子仍然惊慌不安地环顾着周围，突然，她挣扎着坐起来，声嘶力竭地喊道："你放我走！你放我走！……"接着，她伤心地哭了起来。

梅生一时慌了手脚。他连忙上前像哄小孩似地对她说："姑娘，你现在是在月光岛上，你知道吗？这里是个孤零零的海岛，四周都是大海，没有人来伤害你的，你害怕什么呢……"

这番话居然生了效，女子停止了哭泣。她仿佛大梦初醒，脑海里忘却的记忆好似大雾遮盖的景物，渐渐云消雾散显示出来了。她抬起眼睛，疑惑地注视着梅生，一面喃喃自语道："这到底是怎么回事？我怎么会到这儿来了？"

梅生见她开始安静下来，不觉松了口气。他没有急于回

an air of hostility.

After a few seconds she cried out, "Who are you? Where am I?" These were her first words on coming back to life.

"Please keep calm, Miss. Don't be afraid – no one here is going to hurt you." Mei Sheng moved away from the operating table, trying to reassure her with a smile, but she was still alarmed. She gazed around, and then she suddenly struggled to sit up and shouted desperately, "Let me go! Let me go!..." Then she began to cry piteously.

Mei Sheng didn't know what to do. He went closer to her again, and said gently, as though he was speaking to a spoiled child: "Miss, you're on Moonlight Island. I don't know if you've heard of it: it's an isolated island, with the vast ocean all around it. No one will come to hurt you here – there's nothing for you to be afraid of."

His words did produce some effect: gradually she stopped crying. She was like someone waking from a bad dream. It seemed that her memory slowly came back to her, though some scenes were still confused, as though shrouded in a thick mist. She raised her head, and stared doubtfully at Mei Sheng, while murmuring: "What on earth has happened? How was I brought here?"

Seeing that she was getting calmer, Mei Sheng relaxed a bit. He was not very eager to answer her questions, so instead

答女子的问题，而是继续向她介绍月光岛，还作了一番自我介绍。他在说话的时候，用螺丝刀打开一听菠萝罐头，放在她的面前。

她这回没有推却，默默地接过来，用汤匙尝了一口。沉默半晌，她用恳切的口气轻声问道："请你告诉我，我到底是怎样到这个岛上来的？"

梅生的心情十分矛盾。他不善于说谎，可是他也不敢马上把真情实况原原本本告诉她，他担心这个女子脆弱的神经不一定能经受得住这样大的刺激。

女子见他沉吟不语，越发疑虑重重。"难道这还有什么不能讲的吗？对我。"她问。

"不……不是……"梅生吞吞吐吐地说，他见女子一双火辣辣的眼睛直盯着自己，越发找不出合适的字眼来。憋了半天，他只得无可奈何地说：

"当然可以。"他停顿了一会儿，又说，"不过，你必须答应一个条件，我才告诉你，行吗？"

"还有条件？"女子的嘴角浮现一丝不易觉察的微

he went on to describe Moonlight Island to her. He also introduced himself. While he was speaking, he opened a tin of pineapple with a screwdriver and put it before her.

She took it silently and ate a mouthful. Then, after a pause, she asked in a low voice, very earnestly: “Please do tell me how I came to this island.”

Mei Sheng was in a quandary. He was no good at telling lies, but he dared not tell her the truth in detail right now, for he was afraid that her fragile nerves could not stand such a heavy blow.

Seeing him unable to make up his mind how to answer, the young woman had more misgivings: “Is there something you can’t tell me?” she asked.

“No... no...” Mei Sheng hesitated. He was even more at a loss for words when he saw how closely she was watching him with her sharp eyes. After what seemed a long silence, he felt he had no alternative, and answered:

“Of course I can tell you.” He paused for a moment, and then went on, “But you must make me a promise before I tell you. Can you do that?”

“A promise?” There was a very faint smile at the corners

笑，她的笑是很动人的。

“当然，不许激动。不论听到什么，都不许激动，能做到吗？”梅生突然增加了勇气，对她说。

女子羞涩地咬了咬嘴唇，微微点头，算是答应了梅生的条件。她并不理解他的用意究竟何在。

这时，梅生拖过一把椅子，坐在女子对面。他清了清嗓子，扼要地讲起七天前海狼老爹怎样在船舱里发现她的，又怎样跑来找他，从船舱里把她抱上来以及抢救的经过。

“说实在的，你怎么到这儿来的，我也不大清楚。我只知道你是被拖网从海里捞上来的。当时天已经黑了，你又被裹在一堆鱼中间，所以渔夫们把几千斤鱼拖上船，你即刻和鱼儿一起入了库，幸好海狼老爹在无意中发现了你，不过很不幸，当时你早已死了……”

“我死了？！”女子失声惊叫起来。

“嘘——”梅生做了一个手势，示意她不要忘记刚才提出的条件。“你以为我骗你吗？我把你从船舱里抱出来，差不多快九点多钟了，你停止呼吸最少有六个小时（这时，

of her mouth, and he noticed that it was a very charming smile.

With gathering courage, he said: "Yes! You must not get excited, no matter what you hear. Can you promise that?"

The young woman bit her lower lip shyly and nodded her head, wondering what was coming.

Mei Sheng took a chair and sat down facing her. He cleared his throat, and began to tell her the whole story of how Sea Wolf discovered her in the hold of his boat seven days before: how Sea Wolf came to him, how he carried her out of the hold in his arms, and how he had rescued her.

"To tell you the truth," he said, "I'm not quite sure how you got where you were. I only know you were scooped up from the sea by a trawl-net. It was dark at the time, and you were in the middle of a shoal of fish. The fishermen netted up thousands of pounds of fish into their hold, together with you. Fortunately, Uncle Sea Wolf discovered you by chance. But unfortunately, you had been dead for some time..."

"I had been dead?! " she cried out in astonishment.

"Hush –" Mei Sheng held up his hand, reminding her of her promise, "I won't lie to you. When I took you out of the hold, it was late at night, and you had stopped breathing for at least six hours." (After a moment she nodded, looking pensive)

女子若有所思地点点头），幸好你的心脏还有百分之几的微血管没有凝固，动脉、静脉和微血管组织也没有完全僵死。当然，如果在医院里，你准会被送进太平间……”

女子眨了眨眼睛，怀疑地摇着头。“没听说过，人死了还能起死回生……”喃喃地说。

梅生有点恼火，态度生硬地说：“我早就料到了，任何一个人处在你的位置，都会骂我是疯子、骗子，嘴里不说，心里也会这样想的。”说罢，他在房内激动地走来走去。

“你生我的气了？”靠在枕头上的女子见梅生面带愠怒，有些不安。

“啊，不，不……”梅生站住了，用抱歉的口气解释道：“你别见怪，我就是这么个脾气的人。”停顿片刻，他继续用平静的声调，仿佛是向学生讲课似地谈起他的见解。

“要想动摇一种长期形成的世俗观点，哪怕是一个常识性的问题，也极不容易。就以人的死亡来说，这是人们司空见惯的现象，可是谁能正确地回答，什么是死亡的本质，什么才算是死亡呢？战国的时候，虢国的太子突然昏厥

"Luckily, a few of your blood vessels had not yet completely solidified and your arteries, veins and capillary issues had not been ossified. Of course, if you had been in a hospital you would by then have been taken to the mortuary..."

The young woman blinked and shook her head in wonder: "But how can a dead person come back to life again?" She murmured.

Mei Sheng was stung by her evident doubt, and said stiffly: "I have always known that anyone in your position would call me a mad man or a swindler. Even if you didn't say so out loud, you would think it." He began to pace up and down the room.

Seeing him looking angry, the woman leaning on the pillow became uneasy and pleaded, "Please don't be cross with me."

"Oh, no, I'm not!" Mei Sheng came to a halt, and said apologetically, "I'm sorry! Don't be offended – it's just that I'm nervous." After a short pause he continued calmly, like a teacher lecturing his students:

"It's very difficult to shake off a conventional belief formed over a long period of time, even when common sense opposes it. Take the problem of the death of human beings: it's a very common occurrence, but who can say what the essence of death is, or what really counts as death? For example, during the period of the Warring States (475—221B.C.) the prince of the Guo State suddenly lost consciousness.

不省人事，许多御医都诊断他已经死去，宫廷里也准备为太子做后事，发丧，但是当时的名医扁鹊却力排众议，把已经死了三天的太子救活。这个古代医学上的奇迹，用现代医学知识来看，不过是一种很普通的休克罢了。但是，你可以想象，在几千年的时间里，有多少这样并没有真正死亡的人，被那些一知半解、不学无术的庸医误诊为死亡，白白葬送了性命！”

他的声音发涩，说话的调门也提高了。“今天这种情况还不是照样存在，医学还没有从根本上脱离蒙昧的阶段。一个健康的人，突然得了急病，或者遭到意外事故，这种非正常性的死亡和年老丧失生理机能引起的死亡本质上是截然不同的。就像一台出厂不久的崭新机器，损坏了几个零件，完全可以修理，轻率地宣布死亡是不能容忍的！”

梅生越说越激动，没有发觉那个女子突然脸色苍白，呼吸急促。她的头一阵晕眩，身体不由地瘫倒在枕头上。

梅生回过头来一看，不禁吃了一惊。“你是怎么啦？！你看我这个人，对你讲这些干什么……”他后悔地责备自己，

Many of the imperial doctors diagnosed that he was dead, and so the court authorities began to make arrangements for the funeral. But Bian Que, a very famous doctor of the time, prevailed over all dissenting views and brought the prince who had been dead for three days back to life. This was a marvel of medical science in ancient times, but nowadays, from the viewpoint of modern medical knowledge, it is just an example of the common effects of shock. But you can easily imagine how many people were diagnosed as dead by ignorant and incompetent quacks over a period of several thousand years!"

His voice became unsmooth and louder. "Yet such a situation still exists. Medical science still hasn't got rid of its fundamentally unenlightened ideas about death. A healthy person may suffer from an acute disease or have an accident, but such an abnormal death is completely different in nature from that of the aged, which is caused by a deterioration of physiological functions. It's like a brand new machine which leaves the factory with a few minor parts damaged – it can easily be repaired. To declare a death sentence on it over-hastily is unforgivable."

The longer Mei Sheng spoke, the more excited he became, and so he did not notice that the young woman's face turned pale, and that she was becoming short of breath, till she was overcome by dizziness and fell back on the pillow.

He turned his head back and took in what was happening. He was taken aback. He then went hurriedly to her assistance, reproaching himself: "What's the matter? It's all my fault! I

急忙上前扶起那个女子。

“我想问你一件事，不知该不该问？”那女子喘着气对梅生说。她的神色仓惶，似乎有无穷的顾虑。她见对方没有异议，便说道：“按照你刚才的说法，我已经死过一次，而且情况已经到了现代医学无法挽回的地步。因此，我很想知道，你是用什么灵丹妙药把我救活的……”她特别在灵丹妙药这几个字上加重了语气。

“你是不是以为我还要保密。”他冲她一笑，立即转身去取那口盛满蚂蟥的玻璃缸。但是当他走到操作台旁时，他却犹豫了。

“有必要吗？”他想，因为他觉得这里面的动物实在令人可怕。

女子的目光一直追随着他，这时也停滞在那只玻璃缸上。“那里面是什么？”她似乎有某种预感，急促地问。

“蚂蟥——”梅生的话冲口而出。

“啊，原来是这样！”那个女子用几乎听不见的声音自语道。

shouldn't have talked to you like that."

Gradually she revived, but she still looked panic-stricken. She was panting slightly as she said: "I want to ask you one thing, but I don't know whether I should ask such a question." Seeing that he raised no objection, she continued, "According to what you said just now, I have died once, and my case was one that modern medical science would have declared quite hopeless. So I want to know what panacea you used to bring me back to life." She said the word "panacea" with emphasis.

"You think I want to keep it a secret," he replied, smiling, and then turned his body in order to take the glass jar full of leeches, but when he reached the operating table, he hesitated.

"Is it really necessary to tell her?" He wondered to himself, for the creatures inside were indeed very repellent.

The woman's eyes followed his movements, and her gaze stopped at the glass jar. "What's in there?" she asked eagerly, seeming half to be prepared for the answer.

"Leeches," Mei Sheng answered, without further hesitation.

"Oh, so that's how it is!" she murmured, almost inaudibly.

梅生见对方没有动静，以为她并不是自己想象的那样脆弱，便告诉这个女子，拯救她的生命的并不是什么灵丹妙药，而是这种外貌丑陋、令人厌恶的蚂蟥。“你大概知道，蚂蟥这种动物可恨极了。人们下田插秧，它就用吸盘牢牢地贴在人的大腿或者脚踝上，咬破皮肤，同时不断分泌一种特殊的液体，使血液里的血小板失去凝固血液的功能，这样一来，伤口不会愈合，血液就像决堤的河水源源不断流入它的口中。当然，在一般情况下，蚂蟥这种吸血鬼对人类或其他动物都是有害的。但是事物都有两面性，蚂蟥的这种分泌物，具有阻止血液凝固的功能，这是大自然赋予人类的宝贵药物。你想，人的死亡很重要的一个原因是血液在血管里凝固了，心脏接着停止跳动，随之而来的是肌肉僵死，体温下降，就像一条奔腾的河流突然冰冻，停止了流动一样。但是蚂蟥的分泌物却具有特殊的生理功能，在一定的条件下能促进凝固的血液重新溶化，所以我们把这种神奇的分泌物命名为——”

“生命复原素！” 那个女子突然激动地喊叫起来。她

Seeing that this was her only reaction, Mei Sheng decided that she was not as fragile as he had feared, and so he told her that the method used to save her life was not a panacea, but the hungry, disgusting-looking leeches. "You probably know that leeches are abominable creatures. When people are planting rice seedlings in the fields, leeches fasten onto their legs, biting through their skin and injecting a special liquid which they secrete, which stops the blood clotting, so that the wound doesn't heal and the leeches can keep on sucking their blood. Of course, under normal circumstances leeches – like all bloodsuckers – are harmful to human beings and other animals. But everything has two sides, and the secretion produced by leeches is for some purposes a precious medicine granted to mankind by nature, for the very reason that it prevents blood from clotting. You can understand that a very important factor in the death of human beings is that their blood stops circulating in their veins and arteries, the heart stops beating, muscles become rigid, and the body's temperature drops. It's as though a surging river had suddenly been frozen and stopped flowing. But leech secretion has a special physiological property which can cause the clotted blood to re-dissolve. We have called this miraculous secretion..."

"Revivium!" she interrupted, her face scarlet with

的脸色由于兴奋泛出一团红晕。

刹那间，梅生惊呆了。他的脸色陡变，一双眼睛睁得像铜铃似的。

他似乎不敢相信自己的听觉。因为他知道，这个神秘药物的名称到目前为止，世界上只有两个人知道，一个是孟凡凯教授，另一个就是他自己。

他目不转睛地打量着靠在床头上的女子，仿佛第一次见到她似的，同时缓步向她走去。的确，这个女子长得很美，不是一般的美。她长得身材苗条，温柔可爱，一双长睫毛的大眼睛，像一弘碧蓝的深潭，蕴含着脉脉温情；线条柔美的鼻梁下端，一双大小合适的玫瑰色嘴唇紧紧闭着，似乎不愿向人透露她的秘密；苍白得像大理石一样的脸颊上，有一对含笑的酒窝使她的一言一笑格外妩媚动人……

梅生注视得越久，心里越加疑惑。这个女子长得多像他的老师，鼻子、嘴巴，甚至连她说话的声调。难道她……，他只顾这样凝神注视，那个女子害起羞来，极力避开梅生灼热的目光，灵机一动，对他说："我渴极了，给我一杯水吧。"

excitement.

Mei Sheng was absolutely dumbfounded. His mouth fell open, and his eyes were as wide as saucers.

He doubted his own ears, indeed, for as far as he knew there were only two persons in the whole world so far who knew the name given to this mysterious secretion, one was Professor Meng and the other was he himself.

He stared fixedly at her, who leant against the pillows on the operating table, as if seeing her for the first time, then slowly walked towards her. In truth she was very beautiful – unusually beautiful indeed. She had a slender figure, and looked gentle and soft and lovable. Her big eyes with their long lashes were like pools of deep blue water, latent with tender feeling. She had a clear-cut nose, and a well-proportioned mouth – its rosy lips tightly closed as if reluctant to disclose their secret. On her cheeks – still very white – were dimples which gave her a special charm when smiling or speaking.

And yet the longer Mei Sheng gazed at her, the more puzzled he became, for she also reminded him strongly of his former teacher: her nose, her mouth, and even her tone of voice resembled Professor Meng's. Surely she couldn't be... As he stood so long staring at her, the young woman began to feel embarrassed, and tried to avoid his gaze. Then to distract him she said, "I'm very thirsty. Please could I have a glass of water?"

梅生如梦初醒，连忙转身去取玻璃杯。然而他仍然回头向她瞥了一眼，问道："你是怎么知道的？"

女子的神色顿时一变，她的嘴唇抽动，不可抑制的泪水，突然像涌泉夺眶而出。"我怎么不知道呢？"她伤心地说，"我的爸爸就是第一个发现生命复原素的人……"她再也说不下去，俯身在枕上悲伤地大哭起来。

玻璃杯从梅生的手中"砰"的一声摔在地上，砸得粉碎。梅生的全身像电击似地一阵战栗，他不知自己是怎样跑向那个女子的身边，又是怎样毫无顾忌地把她一双手紧紧放在自己温暖的手掌中的。他含着泪喃喃地说："你是孟薇？真的？这不是做梦吧？……"

她的确就是孟薇，孟凡凯教授的独生女儿。她把头紧靠在梅生那双紧握的拳头上。郁结在她心中的万般苦楚，终于像冲出火山口的岩浆，可以向面前这个可以信赖的亲人、她父亲最钟爱的学生倾吐了。她悲喜交加，像见到离散多年的兄长一样，把满腹话语凝集成一句最简单不过的心声：

"梅生哥哥——"

Mei Sheng, like someone awaking from a dream, turned hastily away to get a glass. But even as he did so, he turned his head over his shoulder to her and asked, "How did you know?"

Her expression suddenly changed. Her mouth twitched, and tears started from her eyes. "I know it only too well," she said painfully. "For my father was the first person to discover Revivium." She could not go on, and bent over the pillow, weeping.

The glass in Mei Sheng's hand fell to the floor with a crash and smashed to pieces. He quivered as though he had received an electric shock. Barely aware of what he was doing, he rushed over to her and tightly took both her hands in his warm hands without scruple, murmuring with tears in his eyes, "You really are Meng Wei? It isn't a dream?"

Yes, it was true! She was Meng Wei, the only child of Professor Meng Fankai. She leaned her head on Mei Sheng's clenched fists, feeling that at last she could pour out the whole story of all the bitterness she had experienced, like a volcano erupting, to this trustworthy young man who had been her father's favourite student. She was overcome by both grief and joy, and as if Mei Sheng had been her elder brother separated from her for many years, she crystallized her thousands of words into the one simple phrase:

"Elder brother Mei Sheng!"

孟薇的故事

四年前，一个寒冷、漆黑的晚上……

风刮得很猛，高压线在寒风中不停地呜咽。向海滨伸展的一条松林大道上，寂无人影，显得格外荒凉。

这一带原是T城风景最美的地方，离马路一侧的人行道不远，一幢幢别墅式的小楼，掩映在一片小松林里，这便是东南海洋大学教授们的住宅区。此时，黑暗吞噬了一切。点缀在道旁和庭院中的森森树影，仿佛隐藏着可怕的危险。当暮色浓重，狂风大作的时候，在一扇背景模糊的窗口，却伫立着一个大约十五六岁的女孩子，她的目光呆滞，神色悲哀，一行泪珠默默地在脸颊滚动，那般悲痛欲绝的模样简直使人目不忍睹。

她——就是梅生在月光岛上救活的孟薇。不过比起在月光岛上的模样，她这时要显得年轻得多，脸颊也丰腴饱满些，不脱少女特有的天真和稚气。但是她的神色委实太悲哀了，意想不到的飞来横祸，像夏天的冰雹，把这棵柔

MENG WEI'S STORY

It happened on a cold, dark evening three years before.

The wind was blowing hard and the high-tension wires whined in its cold blast. The boulevard lined with pine trees was a scene of desolation, with not a soul to be seen.

It had once been the most beautiful spot in T-City. Not far away, off one side of the boulevard, was a small pine wood with houses here and there amongst the trees. This was the residential quarters of the professors of the Southeast Institute of Oceanography. At the moment, the wood lay mostly in darkness, and the deep shadows of the trees cast an atmosphere of hidden danger into the courtyards of the houses they surrounded. Looking out at the deepening dusk and the howling wind, a girl of about 15 or 16 was standing still by a dimly lit window. Her eyes were dull, she had sad expression in her face, and tears rolled quietly down her cheeks. She looked unbearably miserable.

It was Meng Wei who was rescued by Mei Sheng in the Moonlight Island. But she looked much younger then, and with a chubbier face than now. She still had the innocent and childish look of a young girl, but she was stricken with grief by a completely unexpected catastrophe, which had hit her like a

弱的嫩草，摧残得奄奄一息了。

事情发生在几个小时以前……

在这以前，这个小家庭笼罩着欢乐的气氛。第一件最叫孟薇高兴不过的事，是她上大学的事终于有了着落。昨天晚上班主任老师家访时，悄悄地告诉孟薇的妈妈，今年的高等学校考试，孟薇名列前茅，取得全校最优秀的成绩，学校打算推荐她上全国一流的大学。为此，母女俩兴奋得一夜未眠。次日清晨，喜事接踵而至，邮递员带来了母女俩盼望已久的消息，出国访问的孟凡凯教授从遥远的巴黎拍来一封电报。

“妈妈，妈妈，爸爸今天要回来啦！”孟薇兴奋得满面通红，一阵风似地扑在孟母的怀里，像撒欢的小猫儿高兴得直打滚。

“都快进大学了，还像个三岁的娃娃，一点不成样子！”孟母被女儿搂住脖子，喘不过气来。她轻轻地推开孟薇，嗔怪地说。

“妈，”未来的大学生撒娇地捂住妈妈的嘴，不让她

hail storm in summer destroying the tender young grass.

It had happened some hours earlier...

Up till then, her small family lived in an atmosphere of happiness. In fact, Meng Wei had extra cause to be happy just then, because the question of whether she could go to university was settled. The evening before, the teacher in charge of Meng Wei's class came round to the house and privately told her mother that Meng Wei was among the best of the students who had taken part in this year's university entrance examination, and that she had scored the highest marks in her school. The school authorities were prepared to recommend her to a first-class university in the country. This had made both mother and daughter too excited to sleep much that night. Then early in the morning the next day came another cause for rejoicing. The postman brought them the tidings for which they had been longing – a cable sent back by Professor Meng Fankai from afar – Paris, who was still on a visit there.

"Mother, mother, father will be home today!" Meng Wei, purple with excitement, threw herself into her mother's arms, like a kitten.

"Behave yourself, and don't act like a baby! And you're about to be a university student!" Meng wei hugged her mother's neck so tightly that she gasped for breath. She pushed Meng Wei away gently, scolding her.

"Mother!" The would-be university student covered her mother's mouth to quieten her, like a spoilt child. "Father's

再说下去。“难道你不想爸爸？爸爸离家都快三个月了，嗯？”孟薇调皮地反驳道，一双水灵灵的大眼睛闪烁出少女的天真。

“死丫头，越说越不像话了！”孟母佯怒地举起手，做了一个吓唬女儿的动作。孟薇却咯咯地笑着，从妈妈的怀里挣脱了。

三个月前，孟教授前往欧洲参加国际海洋生物化学的一个学术会议，并进行学术考察。他的即将归来给全家带来了无法形容的欢乐。孟薇首先想到，她要把考上大学的喜讯，在爸爸跨进房门时头一个告诉他。孟母的心里也有说不出来的高兴。这不仅是因为丈夫远道归来，心爱的独生女儿考上了大学，她的心头还隐藏着一个莫大的秘密，连女儿也被瞒着哩。这天，在她的记忆里，永远是终生铭记的。三十年前她和孟凡凯正是在这天结为姻缘，在海滨的一个乡村小学的课室里举行婚礼的。那时她刚刚二十岁，在小学当语文教员。她无论如何也不能忘记，在她穿上新娘的花旗袍还不满一个月，孟凡凯就搭上一艘开往巴黎的

been away for nearly three months: don't you want to see him again too, eh?" she retorted naughtily, her beautiful bright eyes flashing with the innocence of a child.

"You naughty girl, you're talking nonsense!" Her mother pretended to get angry, and she raised her hand in a mock intimidating gesture. Meng Wei laughed and danced away.

Three months before Professor Meng Fankai had gone to Europe to attend an international conference on marine biology, and to do some research. The news that he was coming home brought indescribable joy to the family. Meng Wei immediately decided to tell her father as he was walking through the door that she had been accepted to go to university. Mrs. Meng's happiness was too deep to be expressed in words: her husband was coming home from afar, and her only daughter was to go to university, and in addition, today was the anniversary of that day, thirty years before, when she married Meng Fankai. The wedding ceremony took place at a country primary school by the seaside. She was just 20 years old then, and a teacher of Chinese. She would never forget that day all her life. Then, barely a month after they were married, Meng Fankai boarded a French liner sailing for

法国邮船，到欧洲去寻找科学的真理了。他先在巴黎求学，继而在布鲁塞尔、哥本哈根和伦敦任教。一直到新中国成立的消息传到大洋彼岸，他才冲破帝国主义的封锁，辗转回到祖国，和离别了十年之久的妻子团聚。

也许是想到今天是三喜临门，孟母从清早起就手脚不停地忙碌开了。她五十岁出头，患有严重的心脏病经常发生心绞痛，这位刚毅的老教师不得不提前退休。可是这天，她像是年轻多了，天气变化带来的不适似乎也减轻了，她一连跑了好几趟菜市场和食品商店，足足从上午忙到下午，当她看到铺着雪白台布的餐桌上摆满了丈夫平日最爱吃的菜肴时，她的脸上露出了满意的笑容。

快近黄昏的时候，天气骤然变冷了。风在屋顶上怒吼，门窗刮得咣当直响，孟薇和母亲不免暗暗担心，唯恐天气会耽误孟凡凯的归来。这时，一阵急促的敲门声打断了母女的谈话。

“是爸爸！”孟薇不假思索地嚷了起来，她的脸颊泛起一团红晕。但是待她兴冲冲地前去开门时，她的手臂被

Paris, in search of scientific truths. He studied first in Paris, and then taught in Brussels, Copenhagen, and London successively. As soon as he got news of the founding of the New China he returned to his motherland, breaking through one barrier after another placed by imperialism to do so, and traveling by a long and devious route. He was reunited with his wife after a separation of ten years. All these memories, however, Mrs. Meng kept to herself.

She told herself that today brought a triple blessing to the family, and she got busy with preparations. She was a little over 50. She had been a teacher, but had been forced to retire early by a serious heart condition. She was suffering from myocardial infarction and angina pectoris. Today, however, she looked years younger and she hardly noticed the discomfort brought about by a change in the weather. She did her shopping at the market, and went to the grocery shops several times. She never stopped working, all through that morning and afternoon, until she saw the table covered with a snow white cloth, laid with all the dishes her husband loved best. Then her face lit with a smile of satisfaction.

As dusk drew near, the weather turned much colder. The wind started to howl over the roof, and blew so hard that the doors and windows rattled. Mrs. Meng and Meng Wei began to feel anxious, afraid that the nasty weather would delay Meng Fankai's return. Suddenly conversation between mother and daughter was interrupted by a volley of rapid knocks on the door.

"It's Papa!" Meng Wei cried out at once without hesitation, her face flushing pink with joy. But just as she was excitedly going to open the door, she felt her arm caught by her mother,

母亲一把拽住了。

她俩迅速交换了一下眼色，孟母急忙用疑惑的眼光示意孟薇："等一等！"孟薇起先感到纳闷，但是不到几秒钟，她也警觉起来，脑子里打了一个大大的问号。

"砰砰" 的敲击声变得更加急促、更加暴躁起来。孟母衰弱的心脏像是被重锤敲打了一样突然感到分外不安。她用手捂住胸部，勉强扶着女儿的手臂，向客厅走去。

"谁呀？"她大声问道。

不料回答她的却是刺耳的、粗暴的声音。"开门！"接着雨点般的拳头落在门板上。

孟薇和母亲愕然了。孟母见女儿脸色煞白，惊慌失措，赶忙用温暖的身体把孟薇搂得更紧，似乎这样可以安全一些，"别害怕，妈妈去看看。"

孟母稍稍镇定了一会，穿过卧室外面一间小客厅。伸手拉开了门后的弹簧锁。

在这一瞬间，两个身穿蓝色制服的人气势汹汹地蹿了进来，卷进了一股冷风。他们没有马上开口，而是用冷冰冰

holding her back.

They quickly knowingly looked at each other, and Meng Wei saw that her mother was puzzled and hesitant, as if to say: "Just wait a minute." At first she could not understand this, but then she too realized that something was wrong. She began to wonder what was happening.

'Bang! Bang!..." The knocks on the door became more impatient. Mrs. Meng suddenly felt very uneasy, as if her feeble heart was being beaten by a heavy hammer. She pressed her hand to her breast, and managed to walk towards the door, holding her daughter's arm.

"Who is it?" she called.

The answer was a loud, rude, unknown voice: "Open the door quickly!" Then fists thumped at the door.

Meng Wei and her mother were stunned. Seeing her daughter become pale and panic-stricken, Mrs. Meng hugged her tightly to her, as though keeping her safe. "Don't be afraid," she said. "Let mother go and have a look."

Calming herself for some seconds, she walked through the small parlour outside the bedroom to the door and stretched out her hand and pulled open the spring lock of the door.

Instantly, two men in blue uniform came roughly in, bringing the wind in with them. They did not speak at once,

目光在母女俩的脸上打量着。

“你们二位找谁？”孟母问道。

“找谁？找的就是你！”其中一个瘦瘦的高个子轻蔑地从鼻子里哼了一句。

“这是孟凡凯的家吗？”另一个有些发胖的矮矮的身材的人态度比较缓和，对孟母明知故问道。

“是的，请问有什么事情？”

但是这两个行动诡秘的人并不急于回答，他们对视一眼，旁若无人地跨进客厅，把孟母和孟薇丢在后面。

瘦高个子背着手来回踱步，一双鹰一般的眼睛四下窥视；矮胖子走到客厅中央的圆桌前，俯身朝摆满菜肴的桌子瞧了一眼，脸上浮出一丝冷嘲。接着他大模大样地坐在靠墙的沙发上，从黑色公文包里，取出一张不大的纸片，放在沙发前面的茶几上。

孟薇还是头一次经历这样的场面。她的目光随着那个矮胖子的动作，一下子停滞在茶几上的那张纸片。她距离茶几只有一步之隔，上面的字迹可以看得一清二楚。当目

but stared mother and daughter coldly in the face.

"Whom do you want to see?" asked Mrs. Meng.

"You, of course!" replied the taller and thinner of the two, giving a snort of contempt.

"This is Meng Fankai's home, isn't it?" asked the other one, who was short and stout, more mildly – though he already knew the answer.

"Yes. What can I do for you?"

But the two men were not forthcoming, and clearly not eager to give her an answer. They glanced at each other, and then walked into the parlour as though they owned the place, leaving Mrs. Meng and Meng Wei behind.

The taller man paced up and down, his hands clasped behind his back, his eyes spying everywhere like a hawk, while the short stout fellow walked to the round table in the middle of the parlour. He bent over to look at the dishes laid on the table, and a trace of a freezing sarcastic smile appeared on his face. Then he sat down on the sofa by the wall, and in an ostentatious manner he took out a small piece of paper from his black briefcase and put it on the teapoy in front of him.

Meng Wei had never experienced anything like that before. Her gaze, following the movements of the short stout man, stopped on the piece of paper he had put on the teapoy for a few seconds. She was only a few paces away, so she could see the characters on it quite clearly. When she took in

光在纸片上停留了几秒钟后，孟薇突然倒抽了口气，双手紧紧捂住喉部，惊吓得说不出话来。

她看得十分清楚。茶几上的纸片是一张搜查证，上面用毛笔写了“孟凡凯”几个醒目的大字，还盖了一个猩红的印记。

屋子里的空气像凝固了似的,使人压抑得喘不过气来。

矮胖子故意用肥胖的短指头把搜查证往前推了推，拖长声调说明了他们的来意：

“孟凡凯里通外国，罪证确凿，已经逮捕法办。现在我们——”他看了一眼他的伙伴，加重语气说道，“我们是奉命前来搜查的，请你们两位给予协助……”

话音未落，孟薇按捺不住地嚷了起来：“你们是血口喷人，完全是一派胡言，我爸爸根本不会做出这样的事情……”她哽咽着，泪水模糊了眼睛，但是她不愿意在这些陌生人面前落泪，迅速转过脸抹去泪痕。

“姑娘，说话要考虑后果，法律对任何人都是铁面无私的！”矮胖子皱着眉头，阴沉着脸教训道。

what was written on it, she was stunned, and had to press her throat hard with her hands. She was so terribly frightened that she was unable to utter a word.

For it was a search warrant, on which the name "Meng Fankai" was clearly written with a writing brush. The paper was stamped with a scarlet seal.

There seemed to be no air in the house, and she felt as though she were suffocating.

The short stout fellow deliberately pushed the search warrant towards her a little with his stubby fingers, and then announced the reason for their presence in a slow but sharp voice:

"Meng Fankai has had secret communications with our enemies abroad. The evidence is conclusive. He has been arrested and dealt with according to the law. Now we have come to..." He cast a glance at his companion, and then continued with extra emphasis, "... search your house as ordered. You will both please co-operate."

He had hardly finished speaking before Meng Wei, unable to bear it, cried out: "You are making slanderous accusations and talking nonsense! My father would never do such a thing..." She stopped, choked with sobs. Her eyes brimmed with tears, but she did not want to cry in front of the strangers, so she quickly turned away and wiped her face.

"You, girl, mind what you say! The law is impartial and incorruptible. It treats everybody the same," the short stout one admonished her, frowning.

“少说废话！”站在墙角的瘦高个子不耐烦地冲着孟母嚷道：“老实告诉你们，孟凡凯一下飞机，就被我们逮捕了。你们要是不老实，那是自讨苦吃……”他向坐在沙发上的同伴递了一个眼色，矮胖子会意地站了起来。

“你们想干什么？”孟薇见状厉声问道，上前挡住那个矮胖子。

就在这时，瘦高个子气冲冲地抓住孟薇的胳膊，狠狠地把她推开了。

整个过程进行的时间不到几分钟，这期间孟母还呆痴地站在一旁，始终没有吭声。她不是没有话可说，更不是默认别人对她丈夫的指控和诬蔑。她的嘴唇翕张，一双颤抖得很厉害的手，在不停地抽动，但是她那衰弱的心脏突然窒息了。她的眼前一阵发黑，一切声音和视像顿时消失得无影无踪……

孟薇听见身后“哎哟”一声，猛地回头，只见母亲脸色铁青，牙关咬得紧紧的，身体摇晃得像一株被狂风拔起的枯木，缓缓地向后倾倒。她悲痛地大叫一声：“妈妈，

"Enough of this nonsense!" shouted the tall thin fellow, who was standing by the wall. He turned to Mrs. Meng, and said brutally: "To tell you plainly, Meng Fankai was arrested by our people as soon as he got off the plane. If you aren't honest with us, you'll be in for trouble too." He nodded to his companion sitting on the sofa, who stood up knowingly.

Seeing their movements, Meng Wei asked sternly, "What are you up to?" and she stepped forward to block their way.

The tall thin one instantly grabbed her angrily by the arm and pushed her aside with force.

All this had lasted only a few minutes. And all the time Mrs. Meng stood on one side, dumbstruck, not saying a word – though this did not mean she had nothing to say. She certainly did not intend tacit agreement with their slanderous accusations against her husband. But her lips were quivering and her hands kept twitching violently, and her poor heart felt suffocated. Suddenly she turned giddy: her sight and hearing began to go...

Hearing a cry behind her, Meng Wei quickly turned, and saw that her mother's face had turned a dreadful livid colour. Her teeth were clenched and her body shook like a withered tree attacked by a fierce wind. As her mother staggered, and then fell backwards, Meng Wei cried out desperately, "Mother,

妈妈，你是怎么啦？”

大约过了个把小时。搜查的人走了。他们到底找到了什么“罪证”，没有任何人知道。屋子里静得出奇，显得从未有过的空旷和冷寂。

孟母人事不知地躺在床上，脸色像大理石一样苍白。孟薇紧握着母亲那双柔软的手，沁出一层薄薄的冷汗，母亲的脉搏忽慢忽快，变得像游丝一般微细了。她心急如焚地等待医生的到来，可是她给急救站打了三次电话，不知什么原因，急救车却一直没有影子……

她轻轻松开母亲的手，试图再催促一下急救站，这时，孟母的身体微微蠕动了一下，紧闭的眼睛慢慢睁开了。

“妈妈——”孟薇全身颤抖着，扑在母亲怀里。

孟母强打精神，半坐半卧地倚着垫得高高的枕头，爱怜地看着女儿，轻轻地用手揩去女儿脸颊上的泪珠。但是她自己却扑簌簌地落下泪来。

“薇儿，你爸爸肯定是遭到天大的冤枉。想起来实在太可怕，你爸爸一生老老实实，勤勤恳恳，怎么会落到如

mother, what's happening to you?"

An hour or more passed before the searchers eventually left. Meng Wei didn't know what "evidence of crime" they had seized and taken with them. The house was very quiet after they left, as though empty and deserted.

Mrs. Meng lay unconscious on the bed, her face as pale as a sheet. Meng Wei sat beside her, tightly holding her mother's powerless and clammy hands. Her pulse was very weak and variable. Meng Wei was anxiously waiting for the doctor to come, but she didn't know why no ambulance arrived despite the fact that she had telephoned three times to first-aid station.

She gently let go of her mother's hands, in order to go and make another attempt to urge the first-aid station to send someone, but her mother moved slightly, and her eyes slowly opened.

"Mother!" Meng Wei trembled, and she threw herself into her mother's arms.

Her mother made an effort to look better, and half sitting and half leaning back against the piled-up pillows, she looked with tender affection at her daughter, and softly wiped away the tears on Meng Wei's cheeks. However, tears rolled down her own cheeks.

"Wei, your father has been terribly wronged. When I think of it, I feel horribly scared. Your father is an honest, diligent, and conscientious man. But how could such a good person

此下场？这样可怕的罪名加在他的头上，他怎么受得了啊……”说到这里，孟母心中一阵酸楚，胸口像被什么堵住似的，满脸憋得通红。她大口大口地喘着气，额角沁出的冷汗把灰白的鬓发也浸湿了。“这是根本不可能的，没有人能比我更了解你爸爸了。我记得很清楚，他在国外的时候，许多著名的大学邀请他当教授，答应给他提供最优厚的待遇和高额的薪金，也可以把家属带来，唯一的条件是改变国籍，被你爸爸断然拒绝了。他给我来信讲，他痛恨那些贪图物质享受而忘记祖国的人，他说，他的知识和才能不是属于个人的，他要毫无保留地贡献给祖国……”孟母用尽全身气力说着，她仿佛预感到有些话如果不及时告诉女儿，也许就再也没有机会讲了。

“你爸爸当年回国并不是轻而易举的。因为他的研究引起了国外的注意，所以他们千方百计阻挡他回国，后来你爸爸瞒过了当局，在几个好朋友的帮助下，冒着生命危险，偷偷地钻进一艘货轮的底舱，化装成船员，才逃出了他们的罗网。这些经历他并没有到处张扬，现在却有

come to no good end? What will he do if there is a serious case concocted against him? How can he bear it...." She was so distressed at the thought that her heart faltered and she fought for breath, panting terribly. Beads of sweat started from her forehead, making the grey hair on her temples damp. "It's simply impossible. I know your father better than anyone else. I vividly remember when he was abroad before, several well-known universities offered him professorships, with excellent pay and conditions and the chance to have his family with him, on the one condition that he should change his nationality. Your father flatly turned down their offers. He said in a letter he wrote to me that he hated those who seek material gains beyond what is necessary for ease and comfort, and who forget their motherland. He said his knowledge wasn't his private property and he had decided to devote it to the service of his country, without reserve." Mrs. Meng put all her energy into this speech, as if she had a premonition that she wouldn't have another opportunity to tell her daughter these things if she didn't do so now.

"It wasn't easy for your father to return to this country, as his research work had brought him to the foreign authorities' attention and they tried by every means to stop him from coming back. Eventually, without the knowledge of the authorities and with the help of some good friends, he disguised himself as a sailor and stowed away in the hold of a freighter at the risk of his life, and succeeded in escaping that way. He never made public this experience of his. And now

人诬告他里通外国，这又是从何说起……”孟母说到这儿，呼吸突然变得急促起来，她闭上眼睛，眼角迸出一颗晶莹的泪珠。

孟薇见状，大惊失色，使劲地摇晃着母亲，大声地哭喊道：“妈妈！妈妈！……”

过了片刻，孟母被女儿的哭喊声惊醒过来。她的嘴唇翕动着，脸颊的肌肉不停地抽搐，她像是在残酷的死神的魔掌里挣扎，依依不舍地拽住女儿的手，用她生命的最后一星火花说出临终前的最后几句话：

“薇儿……我的孩子……妈妈顾不上你了……可怜你……你一个人……孤苦伶仃……往后你一个人……怎么办……怎么办……”

她的话还没有说完，生命的火花便在那暗淡的眼眶里跳动了一下，突然熄灭了。

几天之后，孟薇把母亲的骨灰埋葬在郊外的公墓。这天，天色阴沉得可怕，蒙蒙细雨下个不停，好像她的泪水永远流不干似的。阴风惨惨的墓地，看不见一个人影。她

someone has lodged a false accusation against him of having illicit relations with a foreign country. How can they?" She suddenly became short of breath and had to stop. She closed her eyes, and tears welled up from under their lids.

Seeing this Meng Wei was frightened. She shook her mother with all her might, crying loudly, "Mother! Mother!"

Slowly her mother responded, but her lips writhed and the muscles in her cheeks twitched incessantly: she was struggling on the verge of death. She seized hold of her daughter's hand as if she could not bear to part from her, and with her last sparks of life she uttered her last words:

"Wei... my child... Mother can't look after you any more. I have pity on you – you are all alone, friendless and wretched. You are all alone from now on – what will you do... what will you do..."

She could hardly get the words out: as she spoke, the last light of life in her eyes died out, and she was gone.

Meng Wei buried her mother's ashes in the public graveyard for that area a few days later. It was a gloomy day, drizzling steadily as though it were shedding inexhaustible tears. There was not a soul to be seen in the gloomy graveyard.

跪在泥水里，哭得死去活来，几乎昏厥过去。

“孟薇，不要太难过了……”一个熟悉的声音从背后传来。接着一把雨伞把她遮住了。

孟薇吃惊地回过头来，站在身后的原来是她的班主任老师。她一下扑到班主任的怀里，像是见到了世界上最亲近的人，她哭得更伤心了。

“我全都知道了，孩子！”神情悲哀的女教师把孟薇搂在怀里，温存地捋了捋她沾满雨水的头发，“你要坚强些，孟薇，人死了是不能复活的。现在最要紧的是考虑自己今后的出路——”

孟薇泪汪汪地望着慈母般的班主任。

出路，孟薇是思考过的。在这人生的十字街头，这颗饱尝人间辛酸的年轻的心，还没有对生活完全绝望。眼前还有一线光明，促使她本能地抑制住内心的悲痛，决定要坚强地活下去。

“老师，不瞒你说，以我目前的处境，唯一的出路只能寄托在上大学上。我反复考虑过，反正再过几天大学就要

Meng Wei knelt down in the mud and puddles, weeping her heart out and almost fainting with grief.

"Meng Wei, don't exhaust yourself with sorrow." All of a sudden a familiar voice spoke behind her and she found she was under an umbrella.

Startled, Meng Wei turned, and found that the teacher in charge of her class was standing there. She threw herself into the teacher's arms as though she was the one person left in the world who still loved her, and cried even more bitterly.

"I know all that has happened, my child," the teacher said sadly, holding her in her arms and tenderly stroking her wet hair. "Be brave, Meng Wei. When someone has died they can't come back to life. The most important thing for you now is to think of your path in the future."

Meng Wei looked tearfully up at her teacher who was like a loving mother.

Her path in the future? She had indeed thought about this problem, and in this turning point of her life, her young heart had not yet given up hope, despite her recent bitter experiences. There was still a ray of light before her which helped her to cope with her grief, and she was determined to carry on bravely.

"Teacher, to tell you the truth, I think the right thing for a person in my situation to do is to attend the university. The college term will start soon. I have gone over and over it in my

开学了，管它分配到什么地方，我只要有个落脚的地方就行，至于将来，我现在还考虑不到那么远，过一天算一天……”孟薇止住了啜泣，鼓起勇气，向班主任谈起她今后的打算。她清楚不过地记得，几天前，对，就是妈妈去世的头天晚上，她是从班主任那里知道自己考上了大学的。

班主任转过脸去，默不作声，脸上露出极为凄惶的神色，她挽着孟薇的胳膊，心事重重地走出公墓。在她们即将分手时，这位心地善良的女教师终于开口问道：“孟薇，你在本市还有什么亲戚吗？”

孟薇疑惑地用眼睛瞅着忧心忡忡的班主任，机械地摇了摇头。

“外地呢？”

“没有，一个也没有。我原来有个姨妈，前年也去世了，是得癌症死的。”孟薇答道。

班主任叹了口气。“我马上要离开此地，”她悲哀地告诉孟薇，“这个学校我也待不下去了，在许多问题上，我跟他们的看法有分歧，他们看我不顺眼，我也看不惯他

mind, and so long as I can find a place to stay, I don't mind where I am assigned. As to my future after that, it's beyond my power to think of it at the moment. I can only cope with the present." Gradually Meng Wei stopped weeping and plucked up her courage as she told her teacher how she planned her immediate future. She clearly remembered that it was from the teacher that she had learned, only a few days ago, yes, on the day before her mother's death, that she had passed the university entrance exam.

The teacher turned her head away and remained silent, a very sad expression on her face. She took Meng Wei's arm and walked away from the graveyard with her, still silent as though weighed down with some sorrow of her own. When they came to part, the kind-hearted teacher finally asked, "Have you got any other relatives in this city, Meng Wei?"

She looked terribly anxious, and Meng Wei stared doubtfully at her as she shook her head.

"And what about in other parts of the country?"

"No, none at all. I only had a maternal aunt, and she died of cancer two years ago," replied Meng Wei.

The teacher sighed. "I'll be leaving this place very soon," she told Meng Wei sadly. "I can't stay at the school here much longer. I have so many differences of opinion, on so many issues, with the authorities that they regard me as a troublemaker. I do hate to see the way they do things now.

们那一套。算了，不说这些了，到哪儿都一样，只是我担心你……”班主任说到这里，喉咙哽塞，眼圈也红了，似乎有难言的苦衷。

“老师——”孟薇心里一阵发热，眼泪扑簌簌地掉了下来。

“我很快就要走了，到很远很远的地方去，以后我们很难有机会见面了。”班主任爱抚地用手理着孟薇鬓角的一绺柔发，深情地说，“孟薇，你是个聪明懂事的孩子，在这个时候，廉价的安慰是多余的，不过我还是有几句话要和你讲。”她强抑制住内心的悲痛，暗示地提醒她的学生，“生活的道路是坎坷不平的，尤其是对你来说，今后可能还会遇到许多不顺心的事情。我希望你坚强起来，任何时候都不要灰心失望，不要丧失生活的勇气。记住，好孩子，你一定要记住我的活……”

她再也无法讲下去了。孟薇依恋地目送着班主任老师的背影从视线里消失。她分明看见，班主任扭头离开时，掏出手帕掩面哭泣了。班主任的心里似乎有难以诉说的苦

Forget it – I'll be alright wherever I end up, but I do worry about you..." She couldn't go on; she was on the verge of tears, from some hidden sorrow which Meng Wei didn't understand.

"Teacher –" said Meng Wei with emotion, her own tears starting again.

"I'll be leaving here away very soon and going a very long way away. We're very unlikely to meet again," said the teacher. She gently pushed back an untidy lock of soft hair on Meng Wei's forehead and went on with deep feeling: "Meng Wei, you are a clever and intelligent girl. I know that words of comfort are not much use to you at the moment, but there is something I want to say." She controlled her voice and continued with a warning hint to her student, "Life is always a rough and bumpy road, and it will be especially so for you. You might be beset by a great many difficulties in the days ahead. I want you to be brave: never feel utterly disheartened, and never give up. Remember, my child – you must remember my words."

She was unable to say any more, and thus they parted. Meng Wei was reluctant to move until her teacher's receding figure was completely out of sight. She had seen quite distinctly that when the teacher turned to leave her, she had pulled a handkerchief out of her pocket and pressed it to her face, crying, and Meng Wei had again had the impression that she was labouring under some sorrow or embarrassment

衷，但究竟是什么呢？她始终猜不透。

生活很快把答案告诉了这个天真幼稚的女孩子。不久，高等学校的录取通知书都寄给那些幸运的同学们，唯独孟薇似乎被人们遗忘了。她哪里知道，她的名字已经用饱蘸浓墨的黑笔从新生名册里轻轻地抹掉了，像抹去了一颗小小的灰尘……

几个月后，当T城和外省的许多大学开始办理一年一度的新生入学时，孟薇的邻居发现这个孩子失踪了。不久，东南海洋大学财务处发现孟凡凯的女儿很久没有来领取生活费了。这个消息曾经引起一场骚动，不过过了一段时间，人们寻找她的热情逐渐冷淡下来，就像一块投进池塘的石子，溅起一片涟漪，不久又恢复了平静。

大约过了几年，在一个落日黄昏的码头上，有个衣衫褴褛的女孩子畏畏缩缩地走到售票窗口，买了一张轮渡的船票。她在一个磨损得很厉害的破书包里掏了很久，找出了刚好够买一张船票的几枚硬币，那大概是她仅有的全部财产了。她在穿过很长的摇摇晃晃的跳板时，随手把那个旧书

which she did not want to mention. But what could it be?

Life very soon told this innocent, artless girl the answer. Soon afterwards the lucky students who were going to university received their admission notices, with the one exception of Meng Wei who was apparently forgotten by everyone. She never knew that her name had been inadvertently crossed off from the new students' register, like a small speck being wiped away...

A few months later, when the new students were beginning their courses at the colleges in T-City and other places, Meng Wei's neighbour realized that she had disappeared. At more or less the same time, the finance department of the Southeast Institute of Oceanography noticed that Meng Fankai's daughter hadn't come to draw her allowance. There was some passing interest in this news, but people's zeal for looking for her soon cooled as time passed. It was like a stone thrown into a pond: there was a splash and some ripples, and then it became calm again.

A few years later, on a wharf at dusk, a shabbily dressed young woman timidly went up to the window of the ferry ticket office to buy a ticket. She fumbled as she took the coins out of her very battered satchel, which were barely enough to buy a ticket. It looked as if this was all she possessed. As she walked up the long, shaky gangplank she threw the old

包扔进跳板下面的大海里。

不一会儿，轮渡靠岸，旅客们蜂拥而出，但是那个女孩子始终没有露面。只是在第二天黎明，小火轮上的水手打扫舱房时，在船尾的甲板上发现了一只沾满泥浆的旧鞋，分明是只女式的布鞋。那个水手看了一会儿，便弯下腰，厌恶地用手拾起鞋，顺手扔进了黎明前夕的大海。

“呸！”他掸了掸手，冲着泛起一个很小的水圈的海面……

satchel into the sea under it.

Hours later, when the ferry tied up at its destination and the passengers were swarming out the young woman was nowhere to be seen. At dawn the next morning, when a seaman cleaned the steamboat cabin, he found an old shoe, much stained with mud. It was a woman's shoe. The seaman looked at it for a few moments, bent over and picked it up with an air of disgust, and then he threw it into the morning sea.

"Pah!" He flicked the dust off his hands and looked at the surface of the sea, where there appeared briefly a very small whirlpool.

梅生和孟薇

时间,在充满欢愉的笑声中,飞瀑流泉般地逝去了……

三年漫长的岁月,孟薇在月光岛上可以说过得十分愉快,幸福,无忧无虑。虽然她时常感到困惑,以为自己做了一场无休无止的梦,但这毕竟是刹那间的感觉。梅生像兄长似地对她无微不至地体贴、照料,海狼老爹和渔民们的真诚相待,使她心灵的创伤渐渐愈合了。她深沉地爱上了月光岛,爱上了岛上的新生活。他和她,内心深处都在培植爱情的温床,但谁也没有表露出来。他们默默地期待着,不声不响地期待爱情种子的萌芽。他们只盼望这样恬静、和谐的生活永远继续下去,谁也不离开谁,永远在一个桌上吃饭,一同双双攀登月光岩,一起肩并肩地眺望大海中壮丽辉煌的落日……谁也不来打扰他们。

他们想得多么天真啊!

海狼老爹出海归来,给梅生捎来一封信,他看着看着,眉头皱了起来。

MEI SHENG AND MENG WEI

On the island, time flew like a darting arrow amidst joyous laughter...

For three years Meng Wei lived there, happy and carefree. Though she often felt perplexed, thinking that it must all be a dream, this was only ever a momentary doubt. Her mental wounds healed gradually under Mei Sheng's meticulous brotherly care and consideration, and the kind respect of Sea Wolf and the other fishermen. She grew to love Moonlight Island deeply, and her new life on it. Inwardly she and Mei Sheng came to have a burning love for each other, but neither of them spoke of it. They kept silent, hoping that their growing love would flower without the need to utter a word. They only hoped that this peaceful and harmonious life should go on forever. They were inseparable: spent all their time together, eating at the same table, climbing up the cliff and watching the distant splendour of the setting sun shoulder to shoulder... Why should anyone come to disturb them?

How naive they were!

One day Sea Wolf, back from one of his fishing trips, brought Mei Sheng a letter. As Mei Sheng read it, he frowned.

“谁来的信？”孟薇双手泡在洗衣盆里，问道。

梅生把信递给她，忧心忡忡地说：“局里决定取消月光岛的灯塔，因为这条航线来往船只不多，没有必要设专人看守灯塔……”

孟薇轻轻地“啊”了一声，用围裙擦擦手，接过来信，浏览了一遍。

他们的心情突然沉重起来。

按说，局里的来信是令人高兴的。信中除了通知梅生做好移交工作的准备外，还对他今后的工作作了妥善的安排，也许是为了纠正多年对梅生使用的不当，航运局为他争取到了难得的机会，允许他参加出国留学生考试，而且告诉他，出国考试一个星期后在T城的东南海洋大学举行。他必须提前报到，办理各种手续。

事情来得太突然了。梅生一时没了主意，“我不去了，让他们另外给我找份别的工作，大学、科研单位都行……”他靠着墙，双臂抱在胸前，嘟囔着说。

“你说了些什么呀！”孟薇把洗好的衣服晾在屋外的

"What is it?" asked Meng Wei, who was doing some washing.

Mei Sheng handed her the letter, saying sadly: "The authorities in the Bureau have decided to close down the lighthouse on Moonlight Island because there are so few ships using this navigation route. So they think it's not worth employing someone to keep it working..."

Meng Wei uttered a light exclamation and, wiping her hands on her apron, she hastily took and read the letter.

They both suddenly felt very downhearted.

Ordinarily Mei Sheng would have been elated by this letter from the Bureau, because in addition to telling him to get ready to leave his job in the lighthouse, it also informed him of appropriate plans made for his future. Perhaps from a desire to put right a situation in which Mei Sheng had been badly treated for several years, the Shipping Bureau now offered him a rare opportunity. He was to be allowed to take part in an examination for selecting students to study abroad. The letter told him that this examination would take place at the Southeast Institute of Oceanography in T-City in a week's time. He must check in at the institute and go through the various procedures necessary before the due date.

All this came so suddenly that Mei Sheng was completely at a loss. "I won't go!" he muttered, leaning against the wall with his arms round his chest. "Let them find me another job. I don't care about working at a university or research institute."

"How can you say that?" Meng Wei cast a reproachful look at him. She was hanging the clean clothes on the washing

绳子上，用责备的眼光瞥了他一眼。

“我……”梅生低头不语了，他的脚在地板上毫无目的地踢着。

“多难得的机会,争取都争取不到,怎么可以放弃呢？”孟薇说道。

“可是你——”梅生抬起眼睛瞅了一眼站在门旁的心爱的姑娘，心情矛盾极了。

“你不用为我担心，”孟薇莞尔一笑，宽慰他说：“海狼老爹前些日子说，渔村想办个夜校，给渔民上课，学习文化，问我乐意不乐意当教员。你如果能考上，我就搬到渔村那边去，我想，这个工作我总是可以胜任的。”她故意说得很轻松，但是梅生看得出来，她内心的痛苦并不亚于自己。

“不,我不能把你一个人孤零零地扔在月光岛上。要走，我们一起走！”梅生突然涨红着脸，鼓起勇气把藏在心里的话说了出来。“我早就考虑过了，我们回家乡去，家乡熟人多，找一份工作并不困难。那里山清水秀，风景优美，

line outside the house.

"I..." Mei Sheng hung his head and kicked aimlessly at the floor.

"It's a rare chance, which most people would never get. How can you give it up?" demanded Meng Wei.

"But you..." Mei Sheng, torn by his dilemma, raised his head to look at his beloved Meng Wei as she stood in the doorway.

"Don't worry about me." Meng Wei smiled and tried to comfort him, saying: "A few days ago Uncle Sea Wolf told me the fishing village wants to run a night school and to offer cultural courses for the fishermen. He asked me whether I would like to be a teacher there. If you pass the exam, I can move to the fishing village. I think I'd be good at that job." She pretended to be quite at ease, though actually her suffering was the same as his.

"No! I can't leave you all alone on this island. If I have to leave, we must leave together." Mei Sheng blushed, and he plucked up courage to pour out his heart to her: "I've already thought the problem through. We can go back to our hometown, where we both still have a lot of old friends, and we can both easily find jobs there. It's a beautiful place – green hills, clear rivers, lovely surroundings. We'll go to work

我们每天骑着自行车一块上班，回到家，一块儿进行我们的实验……”他沉浸在美好的幻想中，眸子里闪动着兴奋的光芒：“你说呢，孟薇？”

“不，无论如何不能这样想。”孟薇低着头，手摸着辫梢，深情地说，“不过这是我无论如何也不能接受的，你不能为我做出这样大的牺牲。你的事业还刚开始，路还长着哩。你的研究成果是属于全人类的，拯救千千万万不幸遇难的人，是你的神圣职责，你怎么能够不想想这些，为了儿女情长而贻误自己的远大前程……”孟薇说到这里，又怕梅生误解了她的意思，便亲昵地靠在他的肩头，低声耳语道：“梅生哥，你放心走吧，我等你，等你一辈子……”

梅生的眼睛湿润了，他感激地把孟薇搂在怀里，第一次吻了她。“薇，你太好了。”

离别的日期终于来了。临走这天，海狼老爹一大早就领着他的老伴来了。远远的他就高声喊道：“孟薇，我给你找了个伴儿，你就不会闷得发慌了。”

海狼老爹的老伴五十出头，硬棒的身子骨，乌黑的发

by bicycle, and when we're back at home we'll carry on with the research together..." He was immersed in this idealized picture, and his eyes glowed with happiness. "What do you think of it, Meng Wei?"

"No, you mustn't think like that." Meng Wei lowered her head, and playing with the tip of her plait she said with deep feeling: "I can't agree to your plan. You mustn't give up so much just for my sake. Your career has only just begun, and you have a long way to go. The achievements of your research belong to the whole of humanity; to rescue millions of people who are so unfortunate as to die young is your sacred duty. How can you think nothing of all this, and be reconciled to spoil your bright future for love's sake?" For fear that Mei Sheng would misunderstand her, she came over and rested her head on his shoulder and whispered lovingly: "Elder brother Mei Sheng, I will wait for you as long as I live."

Mei Sheng's eyes were moist with tears as he embraced her tenderly and kissed her for the first time, murmuring, "Wei, you are a darling!"

At last the day came for Mei Sheng's departure. Sea Wolf turned up with his wife early in the morning, shouting while he was still some way away: "Meng Wei, I've brought a companion for you so that you won't get bored."

Sea Wolf 's wife was around 50, hale and hearty, with black

髻，看上去像是四十来岁的样子。她一见孟薇便亲昵地拉着她的纤巧的小手，一面上下打量，一面对海狼老爹说：“我们要是有这么个闺女该多好……”

“亏你想得出来！”海狼老爹啐了老伴一口。

孟薇心里一动，想起一个念头，便对海狼老爹的老伴说：“要是老妈妈看得起我，就收下我这个干女儿吧。”

话音未落，海狼老爹的老伴用拳头在海狼老爹背上报复了几下，“怎么样？死老头子！”她兴高采烈地说。

海狼老爹捋着胡须，哈哈大笑起来。“瞧你美的，还有个干女婿哩！”

孟薇被老人说得不好意思起来，扭头跑进了房间。梅生望着孟薇的背影，当着海狼老爹夫妻俩的面，宣布了他俩的决定：考试回来就和孟薇在月光岛上举行婚礼。他们郑重地请海狼老爹作为长辈主持婚礼，还邀请全岛的渔民统统来欢度这个喜庆的良辰。

“好，好极了！”海狼老爹满脸堆笑，额上沟壑似的皱纹完全舒开了。

hair worn in a bun, and looking no older than her early forties. As soon as she saw Meng Wei she took her delicate hand, and looking affectionately at her, she said to Sea Wolf: "If only I had such a nice daughter..."

"You've got a nerve!" Sea Wolf growled at her.

This made Meng Wei think, and she had an idea: "If you think well of me, I'd like you to adopt me."

Hardly had she finished speaking than Sea Wolf's wife turned on her husband and dealt him several hearty slaps on the back. "How about that then, you damned old man!" she said happily.

Sea Wolf stroked his beard and burst into laughter: "Look how pleased you are! Then you've also adopted a son in law."

The old man's words made Meng Wei feel embarrassed, and she turned and retreated into her own room. Mei Sheng, watching her as she went, told the old couple of their engagement. He said they would hold their wedding ceremony on Moonlight Island as soon as he returned from his examination, and he formally invited Sea Wolf to act as their elder to preside over the ceremony. All the other fishermen and their wives would also be invited to come and celebrate the occasion.

"Fine, very fine!" Chuckled Sea Wolf, his smiles smoothing out his craggy face.

离别的时刻终于到了。梅生提着一只皮箱，踏上渔轮的甲板。海狼老爹拉响了沉闷的汽笛。孟薇的心像是被鸣叫的笛声撕碎了，她拼命地咬着嘴唇，抑制住内心的悲痛。但是当渔轮加大马力，在船尾掀起旋转翻腾的浪花时，她突然产生了一种莫名其妙的孤独感，她泪眼汪汪地望着船上的梅生，仿佛渔轮狠心地把她心上的人抢走了似的，忍不住掩面痛哭起来。

梅生的心也碎了。他第一次领悟到生离死别的痛苦。他扶着船舷的铁栏杆，隐隐听见孟薇的哭泣声。他后悔自己不该轻率地离开月光岛，更不该离开心爱的姑娘。他泪水盈眶，不住地挥手，一面高声喊道："薇——我很快就会回来的……"

孟薇哭得更伤心了……

渔轮当天下午三点多钟停靠在了T城码头。梅生和渔夫们一起在码头附近的一家饭馆里用了一顿便餐。他们约定，十天以后，梅生仍在这儿和他们碰头，搭船返回月光岛。如果有事，可以委托海狼老爹在化工仓库工作的表弟代为

All too soon it was time to go. Mei Sheng, carrying a leather suitcase in his hand, boarded the fishing boat and stood on the deck. Sea Wolf sounded the muffled siren: Meng Wei's heart seemed to be torn to pieces by the sound. She bit her lower lip violently, trying to restrain her grief. When the fishing boat got going, leaving a trail of foam on the water behind it, she was overcome by a feeling of such desolate loneliness that she herself could not account for it: it seemed out of all proportion. She gazed tearfully at Mei Sheng standing on the deck, and murmured to herself that the fishing boat was heartless to take her beloved away from her; then she could no longer restrain her tears, but broke down and wept bitterly, with her hands over her face.

Mei Sheng too was heartbroken. He understood now the agony of lovers who have to part, never to meet again. He clutched the iron railing along the side of the boat: faintly in the distance he could hear Meng Wei weeping. He bitterly regretted now that he had left Moonlight Island so rashly, and even more that he had left his beloved Meng Wei. With tears in his eyes, he waved his hand again and again, shouting at the top of his voice: "Wei – I'll be back very soon!"

But Meng Wei cried more brokenheartedly than ever.

The fishing boat berthed at T-Wharf at about 3 o'clock the same afternoon. Mei Sheng and the fishermen had a simple meal at a restaurant nearby. They agreed with Mei Sheng that he should meet them again at the wharf in ten days time, so that he could return with the boat to Moonlight Island. If he needed to contact them in the meantime, he could send a letter addressed care of Sea Wolf's younger cousin who worked

转递信函。海狼老爹随即把表弟的地址告诉了梅生。

梅生坐上出租车，直奔东南海洋大学。出国留学生办事处设在大学主楼的三层，梅生爬上螺旋形的楼梯，匆匆推开沉重的木门，时钟刚刚敲了五点，离下班只有一个小时了。

几个工作人员正在埋头收拾桌上乱七八糟的登记表格。一个卷发的满脸雀斑的中年妇女，没完没了地抱着话筒谈论昨晚的一场什么电影。梅生忐忑不安地把毕业证书和通知单递给那个女人，她不耐烦地白了梅生一眼，继续对着话筒又说又笑，足足过了五分钟，才把脸转过来。

“你怎么这么晚才来报到？”她瞥了一眼梅生的通知单和毕业文凭，劈头问道。

“对不起，我离这儿很远，交通很不方便，是刚刚赶到的……”梅生连忙解释。

“再晚半个小时，就要取消你的资格了！”她扭动着肥胖的身躯，仍然怒气冲冲地说。幸好她挑不出更多的毛病，待她发落完毕，她拉开抽屉，扔给梅生一张登记表。“填吧，

at the Chemical Warehouse. Sea Wolf gave him the address.

Then Mei Sheng got a taxi and headed for the Southeast Institute of Oceanography. The office for handling the affairs of students studying abroad was on the second floor of the Institute's main building. As Mei Sheng climbed the spiral staircase and hastily pushed open the heavy wooden door, the clock was just striking five. There was only an hour of the working day left.

Inside, a number of people were busy tidying up disorderly registration forms on a line of desks. A middle-aged woman with curly hair and a face much dotted with freckles was talking interminably on the telephone about a certain film shown the night before. Mei Sheng uncertainly handed her his diploma and letter of notice, but she just gave him a supercilious look and carried on talking and laughing into the telephone. Five minutes elapsed before she finished and turned to him.

"Why have you come to check in so late?" she snapped, glancing at his papers.

"I'm sorry, but my home is a long way away from here, and travelling is difficult. I hurried to get here in time," Mei Sheng explained immediately.

"If you had turned up just half an hour later, you would have been disqualified from sitting the exam." She twisted her fat body, still cross. Luckily, she failed to find anything wrong with his papers. And after her crossness subsided, she opened a drawer and got out a registration form, which she pushed over to him: "Fill it in, and make sure you answer each

每一项都要填清楚，我们还要核实调查的！”

梅生没有计较这些，他靠着办公桌的一角，掏出了钢笔。

登记表列举的项目通常是可以想象的。它是铁面无私的法官，使每个人在它面前无从隐瞒任何秘密、任何隐私。梅生的经历和家族实在不能再简单了。他迅速越过许多对他来说是空白的栏目，“唰唰”地写着。当笔下出现“有配偶否，姓名，年龄，工作单位，家庭成员”的栏目时，他手中的笔不由地停住了。

他几乎不假思索，立即填上了“孟薇”这个亲切的名字。他把自己内心全部的爱，熔铸在这个神圣的表格内，庄重地把他生活的秘密第一次向社会公开。他特别注明他们不久要举行婚礼，仿佛他不是在填写登记表，而是向人们发送结婚请柬。他接着郑重地告诉这位公正无私的法官，他的准岳父就是在押的孟凡凯。科学家的良心不允许他有丝毫的隐瞒。他坦荡地写上了他们的关系，并且把从孟薇那儿听来的情况，简要地作了说明。

question clearly. I'll check it afterwards."

Mei Sheng didn't mind. He rested the form on a corner of the desk, and got out his fountain pen.

The questions on the registration form were the usual ones. The authority behind the form was an impartial and incorruptible judge before whom nobody was in a position to conceal his or her personal secrets. Mei Sheng's personal details and family background were simple, and he quickly filled in. He skipped over the questions which did not apply to him. But when he came to "Spouse -name, age, working unit, and family members" he couldn't help stopping.

He wrote the dear name "Meng Wei" almost without thinking. All his love for her in his heart went into answering this question, as he formally made his great secret public for the first time on this sacred form. He particularly indicated that they were soon to get married. It seemed as if he were not filling in a registration form, but sending out invitations to their wedding. Then he earnestly told this impartial judge that his future father-in-law was Meng Fankai, who was in custody at the moment. He had a scientist's respect for the truth, and he honestly wrote down the relationship between them and the details that he had gathered from Meng Wei.

他像是完成了一篇学术论文，从头至尾浏览一遍，改正了几个字，自己觉得满意了，这才递给坐在对面、已经不耐烦的那个女人。

“我们还要核实调查的！”她不放心地又一次提醒梅生。

“没有事了吧？”梅生准备走了。

“等一等！”那个女人突然把梅生叫住，“你的通信地址为什么不填？”她指着登记表问道。

“现在还没有找到住宿的地方……”

“那不行，这么多人，有事情上哪儿找你呢？”

大概是这个胖女人的嗓门实在使人受不了，坐在另一张办公桌的一个年轻姑娘同情地转过身来，给梅生出了个主意。“你填上你家的地址也可以嘛！”她说。

“对了，我在本市还有个临时通信处。”梅生突然想起海狼老爹的表弟，便把这个地址填写在登记表上，让他们有事从那儿转给他。

十天紧张的考试，旋风似地过去了。眼看到了和海狼

It seemed as if he had finished an academic thesis. Then he went through it once more, corrected a few mistakes, and feeling satisfied he handed it to the woman sitting opposite, who was by now showing signs of impatience.

"We'll check the answers!" she reminded him again, clearly not quite trusting him.

"Anything else?" Mei Sheng asked, preparing to leave.

"Wait a minute!" The woman stopped him. "Why haven't you put down your address for post?" She pointed at the form.

"I haven't got anywhere to stay yet..."

"That won't do. There are so many students. We need to be able to find you if necessary. How can we contact you?"

Probably the fat woman's voice was so disagreeable that a young woman sitting at another desk turned round sympathetically and said, "You can put down your home address."

"It's alright, I remember now," Mei Sheng suddenly remembered Sea Wolf's cousin and said. "I have got a temporary mailing address." He filled in the address on the form so that they could get in touch with him if anything happened.

The arduous ten days of the examination passed in a flash.

老爹约定的时间，但是梅生的归期却因故推迟了。

梅生提交的学术报告是关于生命复原素的论文，这项重大的科研成果在学术界引起前所未有的震动，也受到许多当地不少知名人士的注目。一夜之间，这个默默无闻的大学生，突然成为T城上空一颗灿烂的明星。许多大学和研究所纷纷邀请他作学术报告，电台、电视台的记者把他包围住了……

几天后的一个傍晚，梅生摆脱了记者的追逐，独自溜出了旅馆。

他这才想起他和孟薇的婚礼。十几天来，他压根儿把这件事丢到脑后去了。他没有采办一件结婚用品，也没给孟薇买一件结婚礼物，甚至连封短短的信也没有写。他懊悔极了，简直无法原谅自己。

他走进一家装饰着五颜六色霓虹灯的百货公司，像长颈鹿似地伸长脖子，在货架上搜索他的猎物。他的眼睛被各种颜色、质地和不同式样的女式服装弄得眼花缭乱。他的商品知识实在太贫乏。他左顾右盼，想找位售货员参谋

When the day came for meeting Sea Wolf, Mei Sheng was not there for some reasons.

The paper Mei Sheng submitted as his thesis was a description of his work on Revivium. This important achievement of scientific research created an unprecedented stir in academic circles. It also attracted a good deal of public attention locally, and overnight almost this previously unknown university graduate suddenly became a bright star in T-City's sky. Universities and research institutes invited him to give academic lectures, and he was surrounded by radio and TV reporters.

One evening, Mei Sheng slipped out of his hotel, managing to avoid the reporters.

He had just remembered his and Meng Wei's wedding ceremony, which he had completely forgotten about in the excitement of the last two weeks. He hadn't yet bought anything for the wedding; not even a present for Meng Wei. And he hadn't written to her once – not so much as a note. It dawned on him that this was unforgivable, and he felt very remorseful.

He went into a large department store, brightly lit with colourful neon lights. He concentrated all his attention, eagerly in search of what he wanted. He was dazzled by the huge variety of women's dresses – all different colours, styles, and qualities. He knew very little of such things, and so he looked around for a shop assistant to help him choose some suitable

参谋，给孟薇挑选几套合适的衣服。这时，离他不远的一个顾客和女售货员的对话，钻入他的耳膜。

“孟老，你买点什么？”这是女售货员的声音。

“啊，您还在这儿工作。”说话的人声音不高，咬字有些含混不清。他像是在自言自语，“这儿都是女式服装，我要这些有什么用……”他说得很慢，话语中包含着无限的伤感。“这阵子女式服装花样倒真不少，可惜我的孩子……”说到这儿，他突然停住了。

那个女售货员一阵唏嘘。过了一会，听见她小声问对方：“你的女儿还没有音信吗？”

对方没有立即回答，沉吟片刻，喃喃地答道：“这么久了，怕是没有什么指望了。”

“您甭着急……”女售货员正想安慰几句，几个顾客拥上来，她便忙着应付了。

女售货员和顾客的对话，断断续续传入梅生的耳际，他起初没有在意，甚至可以说没有引起任何反应。而且他的前后左右尽是出出进进的男人和女人，使他无法看清那

dresses for Meng Wei. At that moment, a conversation between a customer standing not far away and a shop assistant came to his ears:

"What are you looking for, Revered Comrade Meng?" asked the assistant's voice.

"Oh, hello, you still work here do you?" replied a low, tired voice, seeming almost to talk to himself. "These women's dresses here are all useless to me..." he spoke very slowly, with a very sad note in his voice. "There's such a wonderful range of pretty clothes at the moment – if only my child..." He stopped abruptly.

The assistant sighed. Then Mei Sheng heard her asking, "Is there still no news of your daughter?"

The man did not answer right away. After a moment's hesitation he murmured, "It's been such a very long time I'm afraid there is no more hope."

"Don't give up..." The assistant was about to console him, but some other customers came up and she had to attend to them instead.

This conversation reached Mei Sheng in snatches, and at first he did not pay much attention to it. It even evoked no response in him. And he could not see the customer clearly because of the people in between. However, when the assistant

个顾客的模样。可是当女售货员走到他的对面，这一番对话仿佛重新回响在他的耳畔，他这时脑子一亮，情绪突然变得亢奋起来。

“那个人是谁？他的女儿怎么啦？”他问女售货员。

女售货员一愣，她见梅生并无恶意，便叹了口气，说道：“甭提了，他还是个有名的大教授哩！前几年不知道捅了什么娄子，被关进了监狱，前几天才放出来。回来也是白搭，老伴早死了，一个独生闺女也失踪了……”

“他姓什么？”梅生的心脏差不多快要蹦出喉咙，急促地问道。

“姓孟呀！”她答道。

梅生这时再也顾不上细问了，他来不及向女售货员道谢，扭头向大门冲去，他发狂似地推开挡在前面的顾客，一面高声喊道：“等一等，孟教授，等一等！”

事态的进展如同惊险小说一样离奇、巧合，令人难以置信。

这天晚上，孟教授室内的灯彻夜未熄，不时传来一

came over to him, the conversation seemed to echo in his ears again, and he suddenly woke up and began to feel excited.

"Who was that man? What has happened to his daughter?" he asked the assistant.

She was surprised, but seeing that he bore no ill will she heaved a sigh and replied: "Oh, don't talk about it. He is a well-known professor. Some years ago he was thrown into prison – for what reason nobody knows. He was released only a few days ago, but he came home only to find that his wife has died and his only daughter has disappeared."

"What is his name?" Mei Sheng asked intently, his heart in his mouth.

"His surname is Meng," she replied.

Mei Sheng stopped asking more. He turned, and without even stopping to thank her, began madly pushing customers out of his way to the main entrance, shouting at the top of his voice, "Wait a minute Professor Meng! Wait a minute!"

The chain of coincidences was as fantastic as in any thriller. They could both hardly believe it all.

The lights were ablaze in Professor Meng's room all through

阵爆发性的笑声。梅生和他的老师，不，应该说是和他未来的岳父孟凡凯畅谈了整整一个通宵。当孟凡凯教授听说梅生用生命复原素救活了自己的独生女儿时，不禁老泪纵横，紧紧拥抱着未来的女婿，不知道用什么言语才能表达他的喜悦……

“老师，我一直疑惑不解，孟薇也时常挂记这件事，他们凭什么给你安上个里通外国的罪名？”梅生问道。

孟教授把半截烟头掐灭，嘴角浮出一丝嘲弄的微笑。

“我研究了一辈子自然科学。自信多少还懂得一点科学研究的方法论，这就是详细地、大量地占有第一手资料，确凿无疑的试验数据，然后从中推导出令人信服的科学结论。我想，不仅是我，几乎每个从事科学研究的人，都要毫无例外地遵循这个原则。这是铁的原则。”他习惯地摸了一下满头银发，深邃的目光一直射到梅生的心底，继续说道：“但是我发现我错了，这条原则在另一种场合是不适用的，至少在我们生活中的某些角落，人们却遵循另外一条相反的原则。他们首先制造骇人听闻的结论，而且根

that night as Mei Sheng and his teacher – or rather, his future father-in-law – talked and laughed. When Meng Fankai was told that Mei Sheng had brought his only daughter to life again with Revivium, he could not help being overcome with tears. He hugged his future son-in-law tightly, not knowing how else to express his feelings properly...

"Professor Meng, I have often wondered – and I know Meng Wei has always had the same question at the back of her mind – how did they concoct the charge against you?" asked Mei Sheng.

Professor Meng stubbed out his half-smoked cigarette, and a wry smile twisted the corner of his mouth.

"I have been engaged in research in the natural sciences my whole life," he replied. "So I feel I know something about the methodology of scientific research. You take a large quantity of first-hand detailed information and conclusive experimental data, and then propound a convincing scientific explanation for the phenomena you observe. I believe that not only I but anyone else engaged in scientific research must work by this method. It is an iron principle." He stroked his silvery hair mechanically, and his deep gaze pierced Mei Sheng. He went on, "However, I found I was wrong; that this principle is not followed under certain circumstances. At least in some spheres of life, people use a completely opposite method. They first of all reach a shocking conclusion, and

据这个结论去寻找大量的证据。不过他们是要让你自己的嘴去编造符合他们口味的材料。在你写的文章、书信、日记甚至早已被你忘却的谈话中，他们像高明的考古学家，可以从中发掘各种印证这个结论的材料，于是这个结论，就叫作铁证如山了……”

孟教授告诉梅生，他在巴黎参加国际海洋学术会议时，那是七年前的事了。一次会议休息时，孟教授沿着宽敞的回廊散步，忽然瞥见离他不远的地方有个年轻的外国人，只见他东张西望，脸上露出惊慌不安的表情。孟教授好奇地迎上去，用英语和他对话。对方苦恼地摇摇头，嘴里叽里呱啦地说个不停，显然他不懂英语。孟教授便改用法语和他谈话，这个外国人仍然连连摇头，双手不停地比划，像是有什么非常紧急的事情。孟教授见对方焦虑不安的神情，心里暗暗着急。他四下张望附近有没有译员，但此刻代表们都纷纷离开，回廊一带只剩下他和这个穿着打扮都挺奇怪的外国人了。孟教授百般无奈，只得搜肠刮肚，把他懂得的五种语言轮番试了试，对方仍然像哑巴似地，正在一筹

then go to look for a great deal of evidence to fit that conclusion. They force you yourself to fabricate evidence catering to their requirements. They are like unscrupulous archaeologists, who can excavate different materials to confirm whatever theory they want, digging selectively into your articles, letters, diaries, and even into conversations which you yourself have completely forgotten. Then their selected findings are called conclusive evidence..."

Professor Meng went on to tell Mei Sheng that seven years before he had gone to attend an International Oceanographic Symposium in Paris. One day, during a coffee break, when he was stretching his legs strolling in a broad winding corridor, he had come across a young foreigner who was looking around with an uneasy expression on his face. Professor Meng went up to him out of curiosity and spoke to him in English, but the young man shook his head vexedly. Evidently, he didn't know any English. Then he tried French, but still the foreigner shook his head and kept gesticulating, seeming to want something very urgently. When Professor Meng saw how restless and uneasy the stranger was, he felt worried and looked around to see whether there was an interpreter nearby. However, by that time all the other delegates had gone back into the conference hall, and there was no one else around in the winding corridor: only this strangely dressed foreigner and himself. He had no choice, but tried in turn with the five languages he knew, but still it

莫展之际，这个外国人忽然冒出几句世界语来。孟教授年轻时自学过几年世界语，长久不用大半忘光了。他听出这个外国人懂得世界语，便用笨拙的世界语和他谈了起来。原来闹了半天，这个其貌不扬的年轻人是E国的王子，他和几个保镖第一次到巴黎闲逛，迷了路，大概是昨天晚上的宴会使他肚子不适，他此刻正为找不到厕所而急得团团转……热心肠的孟教授听罢付之一笑，便领着这位王子穿过回廊，到王子需要去的地方去。他哪里想到，他就这样把自己送进了监狱。

“那他们为什么又把你放出来了呢？”梅生问道。

“你大概最近没有看报纸吧？”孟教授苦笑道，“这位王子前不久同他的父亲来我国访问。他对那天在巴黎闹的笑话大概印象太深，所以对我这个中国老头子还有点印象。一下飞机就指名要见他的中国好朋友，他当然不会想到，为了他，我……”

孟教授的眼睛湿润了……

was no good. Then, when he was at his wits' end, the young man suddenly uttered a few sentences in Esperanto. Professor Meng had learnt Esperanto for a few years when he was young, though he had now forgotten most of it as he had not used it for a long time. However, now he knew the foreigner spoke it he began to talk clumsily to him in Esperanto. He then discovered that this ordinary-looking young man was a nobleman in his own country, who had given his bodyguards the slip to take a stroll round Paris but then lost his way. He had apparently been to a rich banquet the night before, and the cause of all his desperation was that he was now urgently in need of a lavatory. On hearing this, the kind-hearted professor smiled, and walked with the stranger along the long corridor and showed him where the nearest one was. It had never crossed his mind that this simple act would get him into trouble – let alone thrown into prison.

"And why have they now set you free?" asked Mei Sheng.

"You probably haven't read the newspapers recently," Professor Meng replied with a forced smile. "That same nobleman came on a visit to our country with his father not long ago. He had not forgotten that silly incident in Paris and so the old Chinese man who had helped him had left some impression on him, and almost as soon as he got off the plane he mentioned me by name and wanted to see this Chinese friend of his. Of course, he didn't know for him I had been wrongly..."

Professor Meng's eyes were moist with tears...

尾　声

海上起了雾，白茫茫的，浓烟般的弥天大雾……

一艘游艇在大雾弥漫的海上穿行，它走走停停，忽快忽慢，唯恐碰上了隐没在浓雾中的暗礁和可怕的旋涡。在游艇前部，梅生和孟教授一站一坐，目不转睛地注视着前方。虽然无情的大雾挡住了视线，使他们看不清百米以外的景物，但他们的眼睛仍然睁得大大的，不能再大了。

月光岛的轮廓终于影影绰绰看见了。灯塔、月光岩、树木……在乳白色的浓雾中若隐若现，似远似近。梅生兴奋地立在船头上，一面向孟教授指指点点，一面指挥船尾的水手向什么地方靠岸。

游艇掉转船头，开足马力，向海湾驶去，它经过那幢石头房子窗下的岩岸，向岸边几株亭亭玉立的棕榈树靠去。

蓦地，梅生向孟教授递了一个惊讶不安的眼色。就在游艇驶过石屋的一刹那，梅生发现临海的那扇窗户紧紧地关上了，而且当他们跳上岸时，没有任何人来迎接他们，

THE END

The sea was smothered in a dense fog, thick as smoke...

Through it, a yacht pursued an erratic course – now fast, now slow, in its efforts to avoid submerged reefs and treacherous whirlpools – half blinded by the fog. In the bow of this boat Mei Sheng was standing while Professor Meng was sitting, gazing fixedly ahead despite the fact that they could see no more than a few yards before them because of the dense fog. Their eyes were strained wide open.

At last they caught the first glimpse of Moonlight Island – the lighthouse, cliff, and trees indistinct in the milky fog. Mei Sheng, still standing in the bow, excitedly directed the sailor at the stern where they should berth, at the same time pointing things out to Professor Meng.

The yacht headed full speed for the bay. It went past the cliff, below the windows of the little stone house, and then sailed towards the palm trees which grew along the shore.

Suddenly Mei Sheng gave Professor Meng a surprised and uneasy look. As the yacht passed the rocks below the house, instantly he could see that the windows facing the sea were tightly closed. When the boat pulled in to shore and they jumped out, no one came out to welcome them – no old Sea

海狼老爹，他的老伴，还有他们的孟薇，一个人也没有。月光岛在大雾中沉默着，木然地凝视着这两个踏上海岛的不速之客。他们像是踏进了洪荒时代的荒岛……

“孟薇——”

“薇儿——”

他俩不约而同惊恐地喊叫着，悠远的、悲哀的回声，从月光岩的石壁，从黑森森的丛林中连续反射过来……

梅生第一个冲进房里，当他走进孟薇的卧室——那间用实验室改作的小房间时，他惊呆了。

梅生记忆中孟薇的卧室，她在这里度过了三个春秋的卧室，那张用木板拼成的单人床，一张临窗的小写字台，还有梅生用石块垒成的堆放杂物的石桌，像梦境似地消失了。孟薇的衣服、被褥，甚至连她的小圆镜子、梳子和漱口杯，一切一切，都无影无踪了。好像月光岛从来没有出现过孟薇这个人一样，孟薇也从未住过这间房子，也没在这儿生活了三年……

梅生像被雷轰似地一阵晕眩，他勉强靠在门板上，半天

Wolf and his wife, not even their Meng Wei. Moonlight Island lay silent in the thick fog, presenting a blank face to these two unexpected visitors. It was as though they were landing on an uninhabited island in the stone age...

"Meng Wei!"

"Wei, my daughter!"

They shouted together in alarm. The rocky wall of the cliff and the shady forest sadly echoed their cries from afar...

Mei Sheng was the first to rush into the house. He was stupefied when he saw Meng Wei's bedroom (once his laboratory, long since converted to her use).

He knew perfectly well that Meng Wei had lived in this room for three years. There had been a single bed made from wooden planks, a desk by the window and a stone table made for her by Mei Sheng with piled-up stones, for odds and ends, yet these had vanished as though his memories were a dream. Meng Wei's clothes, bedding – even her small mirror, comb, and tooth glass – had all disappeared without a trace. It was as though no such person as Meng Wei had ever been on Moonlight Island, as though she had never lived in this room at all, let alone for three years...

Mei Sheng felt as dizzy as if he had been struck by lightning. With an effort he kept on his feet by leaning on the

说不出话来。

“她到哪儿去了？会不会搬到渔村去了？”孟教授吃惊地望着脸色苍白的梅生，轻声问道。

梅生半信半疑地点点头，默默地和孟教授走出门外。他的脑子乱极了，会不会发生了什么意外呢？

满腹疑团的梅生茫然地走着，沿着一条通向渔村的小路，这条路他不知走过多少遍，但这一回却感到如此陌生，仿佛是初次来到似的。孟教授跟在他的后面，突然停住了脚步。

“还没有到吗？”他不安地问。

梅生心里纳闷极了，他们已经不停地走了一个小时，按说早该进了渔村，至少可以看见海岛西部十几间疏疏落落的房子了。但是脚下这条满是砂石的小道渐渐消失了，他们的双脚分明踩在松软的沙滩上，隔着浓密的大雾，梅生和孟教授几乎同时听到了海浪拍岸的声音。

梅生猛地站住，惊恐地回过头来，对孟教授说：“奇怪，我们已经走过了，渔村应该在那边。”他向他们走来

doorframe, but he was unable to speak for several minutes.

"Where has she gone? Has she moved to the fishing village?" asked Professor Meng in a low voice, looking at Mei Sheng's pale face in amazement.

Half hoping and half doubting, Mei Sheng nodded, and then he came out of the house with Professor Meng. He was bewildered: had something happened?

Still filled with doubts, Mei Sheng led the way along a small path leading to the fishing village. He had travelled this path countless times before, but now it seemed very strange to him, as though this were the first time he had been here. Professor Meng followed him, but eventually stopped.

"How much further to go?" he asked uneasily.

Mei Sheng was puzzled. They had walked for nearly an hour, and they should have got to the fishing village by now, or at least they should have seen the first of the dozen or so houses dotted about in the west of the island. Instead, the narrow sandy path was gradually vanishing. They found their feet sinking into the soft sand of the beach. At the same time they could both now hear the waves pounding at the shore through the thick fog.

Mei Sheng came to a standstill, and turning his head he said to Professor Meng in bewilderment: "How strange! We must have passed the village somehow. It should be over

的方向指了指，他的脸色由于惊骇变得难看极了。

他们像大海中迷失方向的船只，继续盲无目标地走着，可是横在眼前的除了浓密的雾以外，便是难以穿行的热带丛林了。渔村消失了，不留痕迹地消失了。

“我再也走不动了，梅生。”孟教授一屁股坐在地上，用手揉着肿胀的脚，他的脸上大汗淋漓，显出十分痛苦的样子。

梅生神情恍忽地停住了，他抬头向前望去。他惊讶地发现，那座屹立在月光岩顶的灯塔，直挺挺地耸立在他的前面不到五步远的地方，他们是怎样走到这儿来的，居然攀登了470级石阶，他完全记不清了。

“这究竟是怎么回事？”他心烦意乱，像是被人捉弄似地喊叫起来。

孟教授昂起头，吃惊地望着他的学生。蓦地，他从地上跃起，两眼瞪得像铜钟似的，大惊失色地指着头顶的天空，用奇怪的声调叫嚷道：“瞧，那是什么？”

他们同时看见了一个不曾见过的怪物在天空缓缓移动，

there." He pointed in the direction from which they had come, his face pale with fear.

They were like ships lost at sea. They continued to walk round uncertainly, but they found only thick fog and the impenetrable tropical forest. The fishing village had vanished without trace.

"I can't go on, Mei Sheng," Professor Meng said at length, and he sat down on the ground. He rubbed his swollen feet with his hands, and his face dripped with sweat. He looked anguished.

Mei Sheng stopped and looked dazedly ahead. He was astonished to see the lighthouse towering before them, not more than a few paces away. He had no idea how they could have got there without climbing the 470 rocky steps.

"What on earth is happening?" He felt as though he were the victim of some appalling practical joke.

The Professor gazed at him helplessly. Suddenly Professor Meng jumped to his feet, his eyes staring, and he pointed at the sky in terror, gasping in a quavering voice, "What's that?"

Simultaneously they both saw a most extraordinary object overhead, moving slowly across the sky. It was a monstrous

那是一只酷似脸盆形状的怪物，周身发出刺眼的绿光、黄光，边沿还喷出金红色的火焰，它一面迅速旋转，一面向天顶移动，隐约还可以听见沉闷的隆隆声。

“UFO！”孟教授头一个惊呼起来。

“飞碟！”梅生的心怦怦直跳。他睁圆眼睛注视着在天顶移动、愈来愈小的怪物，足足看了五分钟，直到它在天际完全消失……

当他恋恋不舍地收回视线时，他一下惊讶得说不出话来。刚刚还是大雾弥漫、混沌一片的月光岛，此刻万里晴空，碧海澄波，像被水洗了似地清晰地展示在他的眼前。似乎有谁暗中施展了魔法。孟教授的举动更加使他惊诧不已。他发现他的老师席地而坐，手里拿着不知从哪里来的两封信！

“这是哪儿来的？”梅生蹲下来，不解地问。

孟教授似乎没有听见，他把看完的头一封信默默地递给梅生，接着又拆开了第二封。

梅生的手哆哆嗦嗦地接过后，定了定神，目光在信纸上移动。他的心情紧张到了极点。

domed machine, the shape of a bowl. Its surface flashed green and yellow light and golden-red flames spurted from its lower edge. It was spinning as it moved. It picked up speed and began to climb, leaving behind faint muffled rumbling sounds.

"UFO!" cried Professor Meng in amazement.

"A space-ship!" Mei Sheng's heart was racing. He opened his eyes wide and stared upwards still at the monster machine which was becoming smaller and smaller. He gazed at it for five minutes until it had completely vanished in the sky...

At last, reluctantly, he lowered his eyes – speechless. And now Moonlight Island, which had been shrouded by a dense fog a minute before, rapidly became visible around them, with a cloudless sky overhead, and around it there were blue sea and transparent waves, clear as crystal. It presented itself transparently before them as though it had been washed with water. It was as though someone were performing magic secretly. What was more, Professor Meng's behaviour made Mei Sheng feel greatly startled. He discovered his teacher appeared to have found two letters. He was sitting on the ground holding them in his hand.

"Where did they come from?" Mei Sheng asked perplexedly, sitting down beside him.

But Professor Meng didn't answer. It was as though he had not heard him. Eventually he handed Mei Sheng the first letter, which he had finished reading, and began to read the other one.

Mei Sheng took it with trembling hands. He tried to calm himself, but he shook with nerves as he tried to read it.

这是一张用公文纸潦草书写的公函，信文不长：

梅生同志：

我们荣幸地通知你，在本届出国留学生的考试中，你的成绩和提交的论文均是令人满意的。不过，你的社会关系是令人遗憾的，它将会成为影响你继续深造的不可逾越的障碍。出于对你的关心，为国家选拔人才，我们再三和你所在工作单位有关部门商洽，建议你对这一问题慎重考虑，权衡利弊。如果你同意上述看法，请迅速函告我们，时间还来得及。

此致

敬礼

留学生办公室

××××年×月×日

梅生刚把信看完，孟教授大叫一声，双臂向空中挥动，嘴里不住地喊道：“薇儿，我的薇儿，你不能这样，爸爸

It was a short letter, carelessly written on official headed notepaper. It ran:

Date –

Comrade Mei Sheng,

We are pleased to inform you that your examination results and the academic thesis you submitted are the best of all those students who have applied to study abroad. However, your proposed family connections are not acceptable, and would be an insurmountable obstacle to your going to study abroad. In your own interest, and in the interests of finding the best candidates to study abroad, we have repeatedly consulted with the concerned department of the unit you belong to, and we suggest that you give careful consideration to the problem before you make a decision. If you agree with the above view, please let us know in writing as soon as possible before it is too late.

Yours sincerely,

Office for Handling Affairs of
Students Studying Abroad

Mei Sheng had nearly finished reading this letter when Professor Meng gave an anguished cry, and with his arms raised to the sky he shouted: "Wei, my Wei, you can't do this.

还来不及看你一眼，你就这样走了……”那种痛苦的表情简直叫人受不了。

“孟教授，您怎么啦？”梅生惊慌地上前抱住孟教授。

“她走了……永远 ……永远……永远不回来了……”孟教授用手捂住眼睛，声音颤抖地说道。

“谁……谁走了？”梅生感到脊背一阵发冷，他连忙从孟教授手里夺过那封信。当他的目光接触到信上的第一行字时，他的呼吸急促，一股热血冲上了他的头顶。

这原来是孟薇留给他的第一封信，也是最后一封信。

亲爱的梅生哥：

我心里有好多好多话要向你说，可是来不及了，我等不到你回来的时间了。再过一个小时零五分钟，我就要永远离开月光岛，离开我们的地球，到那个遥远的星球上去。我永远也不能和你见面，不能和你一起分担痛苦与欢乐，想到这些，我又忍不住掉泪了。

从你离开月光岛，我的心也随你飞回我的故乡，那

You can't go away without your poor father seeing you one last time..." He looked so miserable that Mei Sheng felt unbearable to look at.

"Professor Meng, what's the matter?" Mei Sheng went over to him in a panic and gently supported the old man.

"She's gone – and never, never, never to return," said Professor Meng in a trembling voice, covering his eyes with his hands.

"Who...who's gone?" Mei Sheng felt a cold spasm of fear down his back, and he hastily snatched the letter from Professor Meng's hands. When he saw the first line he gasped, and the blood hammered in his head.

It was Meng Wei's first and last letter to him:

My dear elder brother Mei Sheng,

I've a lot in my heart to say to you, but it's too late to wait for your return. In one hour and five minutes I'll be leaving Moonlight Island, leaving our earth forever, and going to a remote planet. I won't ever see you again – never again share your joys and sorrows. It makes me weep to think of it.

Since you left Moonlight Island, my heart has been with you across the sea, back in my home town of

隔海相望的T城。

我一直等着你，从早到晚，听着窗外的潮水哗哗地涨起，又悄悄地落下去。望着月光岩上的月儿，从东方升起，又在西方降落，就这样盼呀，等呀，等着你回到我的身旁……

这些日子我做了许许多多很美丽的梦。

月光岛上的渔夫们也和我一样做了许许多多美丽的梦。你知道吗？这些天他们忙极了，女人们用木薯椰子酿酒，男人们钻到海底摸海参，捉鲍鱼，找干贝，有的人还潜水去寻找美丽的珍珠……你知道他们在忙什么吗？你一定想象不出，他们是在为我们的婚礼做准备，等你回来哩！我打心底里爱上了月光岛上的渔夫们，你不会嫉妒吧？他们的心地多善良，多正直，简直像水晶一样纯洁。我是下决心给他们上课了，在你出国留学的日子，我就搬去和他们在一起，我教他们认字，教他们唱歌，和他们一道出海打鱼……

梅生哥，我就整天这样陶醉在自己编织的梦里，自

T-City.

I have waited for you from morning till night, listening to the tide noisily coming in and silently going out. I have watched the moon from where it rises above the cliff in the east to where it sets beyond the western horizon, longing for you to come back to me...

I dreamt many beautiful dreams during these days.

Like me, the fishermen here on the island have also been dreaming beautiful dreams. You wouldn't know, but they have been very busy recently. The women have been making cassava and coconut wine, and the men have been diving to the bottom of the sea to catch sea cucumbers, abalones, and to look for dried scallop. Some of them found beautiful pearls... And do you know what all this was for? You'll hardly believe it, but it was all in preparation for our wedding on your return. I love the fishermen of Moonlight Island dearly. You wouldn't be jealous, would you? They are so kind-hearted, so honest, and as pure as crystal. I was determined to help them to study, to go to live with them in the village after you had gone to study abroad. I would teach them how to read and sing, and go fishing with them...

Oh, Mei Sheng, I have been intoxicated with such

己欺骗自己，麻醉自己。

海狼老爹回来了，是一个人孤零零地来到我这儿的。我突然产生了不祥的预感。你没有回来已经使我大大失望，海狼老爹带回的这封信更是打碎了我的幻梦，把我推入痛苦的黑暗深渊……

请不要责怪我吧，梅生哥，我绝不是胡思乱想，我懂得生活严酷的现实，我亲身经历过这种摧残心灵的折磨。我不是也不敢为父亲辩护，也许他罪孽深重，永远应该沉沦地狱。虽然我始终不敢相信这点，可是他的女儿——我，怎么能承担他的罪过，永远无法摆脱这种洗刷不掉的耻辱，哪怕死过一次，也不能摆脱厄运呢？

梅生哥，严酷的现实又要降临在你的头上了，我看懂了这封来信的含义，是的，我不怪罪写信给你的人，他们的心是善良的，他们确是出于对你的关心。而我，你最亲爱的孟薇却不能眼看着你因为我的牵连，影响你的一生，你的事业，你的前程。不，不能，哪怕我死一千次，我也不能让你为我牺牲，付出这样大的代价。

dreams all day long, trying to deceive and calm myself.

Old Uncle Sea Wolf came back at last, but he came back alone and when he came to see me I had ominous forebodings. I was terribly disappointed that you hadn't come back with him. Then he gave me the letter he'd brought back with him, which shattered all my dreams and drove me to the depths of agony...

Don't blame me, elder brother Mei Sheng. I do not imagine things, for I understand the harsh realities of life only too well, and I have experienced heart-breaking suffering. I do not and dare not plead for my father, for he might really be guilty and should sink into degradation forever. I don't believe it from beginning to end – how can I? But if it's true, as his daughter, what sin have I committed that I should be responsible for what my father has done? And I can never escape misfortune – even though I've already died once.

Elder brother Mei Sheng, harsh reality has claimed you. I understand very well the implications of the authorities' letter to you. I don't blame those who wrote it, for they are kind-hearted and wrote to you simply out of concern for you. And I, your dearest Meng Wei, cannot let your life, your career, and your future be jeopardized by your connection with me. No, I can't do that. If I had to die a thousand times, I would not let you sacrifice so much and pay so dearly for my sake.

梅生哥，其实我应该满足，当我冷静下来的时候，我这样想。我感谢你继承了父亲的事业，也感谢你用生命复原素救活了我。这令人难忘的三年，你留给我的美好回忆足以补偿我过去的辛酸。我该知足了，不能奢望我不该得到的幸福。在这和你永远诀别的时刻，我只有一种心愿，我希望你把这项科学研究继续下去，拯救千千万万不幸的男人、女人和可爱的孩子，我想，父亲身陷囹圄也会感到莫大的安慰。

梅生哥，永别了，但不要以为我会走上绝路，重蹈上次的覆辙。当然我曾经萌生过这个愚蠢的念头，我偷偷摆脱了时刻不敢离开我的老妈妈——海狼老爹的老伴，跑上了月光岩，可是就在我纵身跳下时，老妈妈从背后抱住了我，我欲生不能，欲死不能，只好悲伤地嚎啕大哭……

“孩子，我们都知道了！”不知什么时候海狼老爹和许多渔夫都赶来了，他们一个个怒不可遏，眼里喷射出愤怒的火焰，对我的遭遇十分同情。海狼老爹对我说：“孟薇，我的女儿，跟我们走吧，远远地离开这儿！”

I ought to be happy, elder brother Mei Sheng, and I will be when I am calmer. You carry on my father's career, and you brought me back to life again with Revivium. I owe you my whole existence. These three unforgettable years have left me so many happy memories that they more than make up for my previous sorrows. I should be content, and therefore, I should not cherish extravagant hopes for an impossible happiness. As I approach the time to leave, never to meet you again, I have only one hope, which is that you will carry on your scientific research and save thousands of unfortunate man, women and lovely children. I think in this way my father, even though in prison, would feel greatly comforted.

Elder brother Mei Sheng, farewell forever. Don't think I'm going to commit suicide again, though it's true that I've thought of it. One day I secretly shook off old Auntie – Uncle Sea Wolf's wife, who stayed with me all the time – and climbed up to the cliff. But as I was about to jump, old Auntie held me tight from behind and stopped me from dying. But I didn't want to live, and cried my eyes out in my misery...

Then someone said: "My child, we know all about it." And I found that Uncle Sea Wolf and several of the other fishermen were standing round me. They'd come up without my noticing it. They were all very angry on my behalf, and sympathized with my hard lot. Uncle Sea Wolf said to me, "Meng Wei, my daughter, leave here and come with us to our faraway home."

“你们？到哪儿去？”我小声地问。我的心里十分惶惑，不明白海狼老爹说的是什么意思。

他们大概猜出了我的疑虑，互相望着，会意地笑了。

忽然，海狼老爹用一种我听不懂的语言和大家说了些什么，他们互相商量了一会儿，他们说话的内容我完全不理解，但从他们严肃的表情中可以判断，他们商量的是件十分重大的事情，而且和我有关。

过了片刻，大家赞同地点点头，脸上露出非常高兴的表情，甚至有人情不自禁地拍起巴掌来了。

海狼老爹走到我的身边，用我们的语言对我说道：“我的女儿，我现在要坦率地告诉你，我们都不是地球人，我们更不是渔夫。你也许听说过，在距离地球很遥远的宇宙空间有一颗美丽无比的天狼星，那就是我们的家乡。我们是自由的天狼星人。我们35个天狼星人自愿结合，组成了一支考察队，我们都是对地球有着浓厚兴趣的科学家和大学教授。”他说罢，把站在我周围的渔夫们，不！是天狼星人向我作了介绍，他们的名

"Why, where are you going?" I asked in a low voice, very much perplexed. I couldn't understand what Sea Wolf meant.

They understood my bewilderment, and smiled knowingly at each other.

Then Uncle Sea Wolf suddenly said something to the others in a language I didn't know, and they talked for some while. I couldn't understand in the least what they were saying, but judging by their solemn expressions, they were discussing a very important matter which seemed to concern me.

At last the others nodded in approval, their faces beaming. Some of them even clapped their hands.

Uncle Sea Wolf came over to me and said in our own language, "My daughter, I must now tell you the truth. We are not human beings, still less fishermen. You may have heard that very far away from this earth is an incomparably beautiful planet called Sirius. Well, we're from there. We are free Sirius people, all 35 of us – volunteers who formed a survey team. We are all scientists and researchers who have a great interest in the earth," having said that, he introduced me to the fishermen one by one – or rather, to the Sinus people. Their names were extraordinarily long,

字都长得出奇，我简直无法记住。不过我还是好不容易记住了我老妈妈的名字，她叫契阿伯勒官格尔斯特卡尔玛，是天狼星上首屈一指的地球生物艺术史的专家。

我惊讶极了。海狼老爹，不，他是著名的天狼星科学院院士。他大概看出我的疑惑，便主动向我解释。他们在地球上考察了十年，收集了大量的资料，经过实地考察，他们推翻了天狼星人过去沿袭下来的对地球人的传统看法，据说那是他们的一位先哲所作的结论，那位先哲认为地球人是比天狼星人更高级、更文明、进化程度更高的、伟大的生物群。

“我们尊重伟大的先哲，但是他的结论是我们无法接受的。”这位老院士严峻地说，“所以我们要马上回去，把我们考察的结果告诉我们的同胞，他们是非常乐于接受新思想、新见解的。”

我忘记了自己的身份，也忘记了自己的处境，不禁好奇地问：“你们认为地球人如何呢？”

“请原谅，当着你的面讲也许是不礼貌的。”这位

and I found it hard to remember them, but with a great effort I managed to get my good Mother's name. She is called Chiabra- gongalstekalma, and is their top expert on the History of Art of the Living Beings of the Earth.

I was astounded. Uncle Sea Wolf, who is in fact a well-known academician of the Sirius Academy of Sciences, probably saw that I was bewildered, and explained a bit more. They have been conducting research on the earth for ten years, and have collected large quantities of data. From their on-the-spot investigations they have found that the traditional beliefs about earth people held by the Sirusians are incorrect. It was said that a sage of theirs had concluded that the human beings on earth were a great living group more advanced, more civilized, and more evolutionarily advanced than the Sirusians.

"We respect the great sage, but his conclusions are wrong," the old academician told me solemnly. "We're going back now, to tell our compatriots about our findings. They are always ready to accept new ideas and new viewpoints."

I forgot myself and my troubles for a moment, and asked curiously, "What do you think of the human beings on earth?"

"I must beg your pardon, for you might think me rude if I tell you our opinion of mankind," he said apologetically,

老人突然歉意地说："请恕我直言，地球人要进入文明的理想境界，大约需要再经过一百个世纪。根据我们的研究，他们比起宇宙中其他星球的人，无论是科学技术，还是社会公德都差得太远太远……"

这时，好心的老妈妈向她的丈夫使了一个眼色，责备道："你何必当着她的面说这些！"接着她转脸对我说，"女儿，你别生气，他并没有指某一个地球人，这仅仅是一种哲学上的、抽象化的概念而已……"

"不，好妈妈，你不必解释了。"我拉着她的手，说道，"真理往往一开始总是不容易被人接受的……"

他们听见我这样说全都满意地点点头。

梅生哥，以后的事情我就不必和你细谈了，时间来不及了。我接受了他们的邀请，和他们一道飞向遥远的天狼星。现在大雾已经笼罩了月光岛，那是他们的飞船正在着陆，再过一刻钟，我们就要乘这艘来自天狼星的飞船，永远离开地球，我们留在地球上的一切痕迹也将随着飞船的离去自动消失。

"so excuse me for speaking bluntly: but the human race will need another 100 centuries before it reaches an ideal state of civilization. According to our research they still have a long way to go compared with the inhabitants of other celestial bodies in outer space, whether in science, in technology, or in social morality..."

Then my kind old Auntie interrupted her husband and ticked him off, saying, "You shouldn't say such things to her." She turned to me and said, "My daughter, don't get angry with him. He didn't intend to refer to any particular human being; he was talking about philosophical and abstract concepts..."

"Don't worry, dear Mother, I understand," I said. Then I took her hand and added, "At first people often find it hard to accept the truth."

On hearing my words they all nodded in satisfaction.

Elder brother Mei Sheng, there is no need for me to tell you in detail all the events that followed, and anyway I'm running out of time. I have decided to accept their invitation to go with them to Sirius. Now a thick fog is covering Moonlight Island and it's time for their spaceship to land. In a quarter of an hour we'll get on board and leave the earth forever. All traces of us on the earth will disappear automatically with the departure of the spaceship.

永别了，他们正在呼唤我。梅生哥，我希望你答应我最后一个请求：

忘掉我，自己坚强地活下去。要记住，科学需要你献身。

啊！飞船快起飞了，我要走了！

终生爱你的薇

于月光岩上

梅生沉默了。他手里紧紧攥着孟薇的信，长久地仰望着万里碧空。那里有一只雄鹰展翅翱翔。几朵白色的云彩凝固不动，像睡着了似的。不知名的热带花朵在岩缝里怒放，随风飘来阵阵幽香，海浪不知疲倦地拍打着沙滩，唱着安详的催眠曲。这一切仿佛告诉他，地球从来是这样和谐、美好，似乎什么事情都没有发生过。

梅生望了神思恍惚的孟教授一眼，用手摇了摇他的肩膀，“孟教授，我们回去吧！”他口气坚决地说。

“那她……她呢？”孟教授不曾睡醒似地，嘟哝着。

Farewell to you. They are calling me. Elder brother Mei Sheng, please make me one last promise:

Forget me, and live on bravely. Remember, science needs you to give your life for it.

Oh! The spaceship is going to take off. We are about to leave.

Your life-long devoted Wei,
On Moonlight Island.

Mei Sheng was silent. He stared into the blue sky for a long time, clutching Meng Wei's letter. There was a noble eagle soaring overhead, and there were several white clouds as motionless as if they had fallen asleep. Around him, the nameless wild tropical flowers were in full bloom, giving a delicate fragrance to the air with the wind. The waves beat ceaselessly against the sandy beach, singing a serene lullaby. All these things showed him an earth as harmonious and beautiful as if nothing had happened.

At last he looked across at Professor Meng, who was still sitting in a trance, and then he shook his shoulder. "Let's go home, Professor Meng," he said resolutely.

"What... what about her?" Professor Meng murmured, as though he were still half asleep.

“走了，她走得好！”梅生咬着嘴唇，头也不回地跑下月光岩。

他跑得飞快，灯塔、月光岩以及往事的记忆都远远甩在他的背后了……

“She’s gone. It was better for her to leave us.” Mei Sheng bit his lower lip, and then he started down the long flight of rocky steps without turning his head back.

He was running so fast that the lighthouse, the cliff, and his memories of the past were all left far behind...

作者简介

金涛 科普作家、科幻小说家、高级编辑。1940年生，祖籍安徽黟县，世居江西九江。1957年入北京大学。曾任报社编辑、记者，出版社社长、总编辑。中国科普作家协会副理事长，中国作家协会会员。现已退休。

主要作品有科幻小说《月光岛》《台风行动》《冰原迷踪》《失踪的机器人》《马小哈奇遇记》，童话《谁是凶手》《大海妈妈和她的孩子们》和散文《暴风雪的夏天》等。

1984～1985年参加中国首次南极考察，被国家南极考察委员会授予二等功。1991年7月获范长江新闻奖提名荣誉。1996年被国家科委等部门授予全国先进科普工作者称号。

About the author

Jin Tao is a popular science writer, SF writer, senior editor. He was born in 1940. His ancestral home is in Yixian County of Anhui Province, but his family has settled down in Jiujiang of Jiangxi Province for generations. Began to study at Being University in 1957. Had been newspaper editor, reporter, publishing house head and chief-editor. Vice-chairman of Popular Science Writers Association, member of Chinese Writers Association. Now Jin has retired.

Jin's principal works include SF works: *Moonlight Island, Typhoon Action, Getting Lost in the Iceland, The Lost Robot, The Adventure of Maxiaoha*; fables: *Who is the Murderer, Mother Ocean and her Children*; essay: *Snowstorm in Summer*; etc.

Jin took part in China's first Antarctic Pole investigation in 1984—1985, and was conferred Merit Citation Class II by the Antarctic Pole Investigation Committee; nominee for Fan Changjiang News Award in July, 1991; conferred the title National Advanced Popular Science Worker by the State Science and Technology Commission and other state organs.

译者简介

温绍贤 生于香港，早年毕业于中山大学西方语言文学系。温绍贤是资深翻译家和中英文编辑，翻译和译审的书籍超过100部；他还是长期从事英汉语言比较和翻译研究的学者，有多部学术专著问世；他同时又是小说作家，擅长撰写政经历史长篇小说，代表作有《红的回忆》五部曲和“绿印人”系列三部短篇小说集。现任郑州大学西亚斯国际学院荣誉教授。

在中国图书对外推广网和中国作家协会共同建立的“翻译名家”和“作家档案”网上，均有介绍温绍贤的条目。

有关温绍贤生平的详情，请参阅网上“维基百科”对他的介绍。

英文文字编辑简介

蒂娜·巴莱（Tina Bailey），资深英文译审。

About the translator

Wen Shaoxian was born in Hong Kong. He graduated from the Department of Western Languages and Literature at Sun Yat-sen University. He is a veteran translator as well as a professor of translation and comparative grammar. He has translated and copy-edited more than 100 books of different disciplines. Now Wen is honorary professor with SIAS international University in Central China.

Wen is also a literary writer, expert in writing political and historical novels. His representative works include *Red Memories* pentalogy and *New Immigrants*, a series of three short story collections.

About the English copy–editor

Tina Bailey, veteran English copy-editor.